CIVILIZATION AND ITS DISCONTENTED

In Memory of Sanford Elwitt (January 18, 1936—May 11, 1988)

Colleague, Friend, Comrade.

CIVILIZATION AND ITS DISCONTENTED

John F. Laffey

Montréal/New York/London

BLACK ROSE BOOKS No. W196
Hardcover ISBN 1-895431-71-9
Paperback ISBN 1-895431-70-0

Library of Congress No. 93-70388

Canadian Cataloguing in Publication Data

Laffey, John F.
Civilization and its discontented

ISBN 1-895431-71-9 (bound) –
ISBN 1-895431-70-0 (pbk.)

1. Civilization. 2. Alienation (Social psychology). 3. Freud, Sigmund,
1856-1939—Views on civilization. I. Title.

CB19.L25 1993   909   C93-090099-5

Cover design: Nat Klym

Mailing Address

BLACK ROSE BOOKS   BLACK ROSE BOOKS
C.P. 1258   340 Nagel Drive
Succ. Place du Parc   Cheektowaga, New York
Montréal, Québec   14225 USA
H2W 2R3 Canada

Printed in Canada

A publication of the Institute of Policy Alternatives of Montréal
(IPAM)

CONTENTS

PREFACE

MANY HISTORIANS have difficulty with notions and terms now fashionable among their more theoretically-inclined colleagues in other disciplines. Words like "logocentric," "phallocratic" and "postmodern" strike many of them as weapons in the cultural wars of the present rather than as useful tools for the investigation of the past. Whatever their politics, historians have to be numbered among the more conservative academic breeds: the facts, however defined, selected and interpreted, constrain. But such conservatism is not without danger: the familiar can go unexamined. Such seems to be the case with "civilization," a term which the linguist Emile Benveniste ranked among the "few dozen words" central to the whole history of modern thought."[1] While the stuff of innumerable course and textbook titles, of dictionary and encyclopedia entries, the complexities of civilization's usage, especially its ideological usage, have seldom received the attention they deserve.[2]

The following essays constitute the prolegomena to a much larger study of the same subject. The passage of time, the realization of the inexhaustibility of the subject, and competing interests determined me to publish these essays now. The first follows civilization from its emergence as a normative concept late in the eighteenth century to its reformulation in 1930 by Sigmund Freud. Although never without challenge, the idea gained a hegemonic status in the nineteenth century which ultimately would be severely shaken by World War I. Remarkably capacious, it was open to a variety of definitions and usages. While national differences intruded into its interpretation, the basic questions in regard to it remained much the same: did its essence, as the Enlightenment believed, lie in a refinement of manners; or in Christianity and, if so, in which variety thereof; or in industry and commerce; or in science and technology; or in urban life; or in the "progress" and/or "modernity" used to sum up several or even all of these factors? Allied to the questions having to do with civilization's intrinsic qualities were others which had to do with its relation to "culture," its status as process and/or state, its liability to decay, its "artificiality" in relation to "Nature," its antitheses and the borderlands which separated it from those antitheses.

The second essay addresses that last issue, that is, the groups who were either relegated to civilization's margins or cast beyond its pale: the "savages" abroad or on the frontier and, at home, the labouring classes, criminals, the insane, urban crowds and women. Such groups, frequently equated with each other, failed to measure up to the standards of civilization established and ceaselessly invoked by those, usually bourgeois professional men, who believed that they had proven their distance from and superiority to brute Nature by means of intellect, will power, dedication to hard work, and a self-control which gave them the right to exercise control over others whose very discontents signalled their distance from civilization.

The third essay seeks to place Freud, who grappled with the problem of civilization from very early in his career, within this tradition of discourse. While the problem itself was by no means new, his striking reformulation of it better served the ideological needs of his grim times than did the shibboleths of the nineteenth century which had been so badly shaken by World War I. Bringing the idea of civilization together with his more general view of human nature, Freud achieved a new articulation of a tradition which had begun with Thomas Hobbes in the seventeenth century and, in that sense, he may well have been the last of the great bourgeois ideologists. Strictly historical, none of these essays carries the story beyond 1930, the year in which he published *Civilization and Its Discontents*.

All of the essays are focused upon the ideological uses to which stereotypes have been put. As every ideology involves a greater or lesser degree of distortion of reality, these stereotypes tell much more about those doing the judging, in light of the purported standards of civilization, than they do about the judged. However much their social superiors would like them to be so, the dominated are never simply objects to be described, classified, coerced and manipulated. Complex beings, neither the Victorian housewife nor the Victorian prostitute corresponded completely to the images formulated by male commentators. The same could be said of the working class or Amerindians. These "Others" fought back, sometimes in extraordinarily subtle fashions. This is not to suggest, however, that stereotypes did not have an impact upon the lives of those to whom they were applied. With stereotypes entering into matters as different as government policies and medical practice, they did have influence, not least when those to whom they were applied tried to live up or down to them. While never completely reflecting reality, stereotypes did play a role in structuring historical environments which, in turn, generated discontents which often enough worked to confirm them in the minds of those who held them.

Further cautions are in order. Two groups often introduced into the equation process, children and animals, will not be treated here. But two points can be made about them. First, the stereotypes of the child, like that of the woman, ranged from the angelic to the demonic. Second, the demonic often turned into the bestial. As for the latter dimension, it was John Stuart Mill, very much a cultural liberal in regard to his own society, who remarked: "The state of different communities, in point of culture and development, ranges downwards to a condition very little above the highest of the beasts."[3] As that kind of thinking has not disappeared, these studies, while strictly historical in nature, have a bearing on the contemporary situation, for the unjustly judged and legitimately discontented are still very much with us, a matter which will be treated briefly in the conclusion.

If we all harbour discontents of various sorts, I can hardly complain, for I have been remarkably favoured. Whatever the solitude of the study, scholarship is a collective enterprise. As the notes indicate, I have depended heavily on the work of scholars in fields other than my own. Moreover, I have been extraordinarily fortunate in those who over the years have encouraged me in one fashion or another. Fortunate in my teachers, especially Knight Biggerstaff. Fortunate in my students, notably Andrea Levy. Fortunate in colleagues at Concordia University, particularly Alan Adamson and Franziska Shlosser. Fortunate in my colleagues elsewhere, notably Michel Grenon and Camille Limoges at UQAM and, at a further remove, Mary M. Rowan of Brooklyn College. Fortunate in having taught with and learned from that master of the historical craft and firm anti-Fascist, the late George Rudé. Fortunate in my friends from outside the academic world, especially Svetlana Bychkova and Aïda Nagy. My greatest debts, debts which cannot be fully expressed, let alone repaid, are owed to Shirley Ascroft. These essays are dedicated to the memory of this historian's ideal of the historian.

NOTES

1. Emile Benveniste, *Problems in General Linguistics* (Coral Gables: University of Miami Press, 1971), p. 289. Benveniste's "modern" is as important and poses even more problems than "civilization." Often the two terms have been yoked together. See John F. Laffey, "Cacophonic Rites: Modernism and Postmodernism," *Historical Reflections / Réflexions historiques*, 14, 1 (Spring, 1987), pp. 1-32.

2. But see Philippe Bénéton, *Histoire des Mots: culture et civilisation* (Paris: Presses de la Fondation national des Sciences politiques, 1975); Norbert Ellias, *The Civilizing Process*, 2 vols. (New York: Pantheon Books, 1978, 1982); and "Civilization: evolution of a word and a group of ideas," Peter Burke (ed.), *A New Kind of History: From the Writings of Lucien Febvre* (London: Routledge and Kegan Paul, 1973), pp. 219-57. As will become apparent, the problem of culture has often overlapped with that of civilization. For very different approaches, see A. L. Kroeber and Clyde Kluckhohn, *Culture: A Critical Review of Concepts and Definitions* (New York: Vintage Books, n.d.) and Christopher Herbert, *Culture and Anomie: Ethnographic Imagination in the Nineteenth Century* (Chicago: University of Chicago Press, 1991). See also the following works by Raymond Williams; *Culture and Society, 1780-1950* (Harmondsworth: Penguin Books, 1961); "Culture and Civilization," Paul Edwards (ed.) *The Encyclopedia of Philosophy*, II (New York: Macmillan, 1967), pp. 273-76; and *Keywords: A Vocabulary of Culture and Society* (New York: Oxford University Press, 1983).

3. "Representative Government," John Stuart Mill, *Utilitariansim, Liberty, Representative Government* (New York: E. P. Dutton, 1951), p. 264. When it came to civilization, Mill remained very much the liberal (and not altogether, paradoxically, the loyal servant of the East India company). Hence, he maintained that "uncivilized races, and the bravest and most energetic still more than the rest, are adverse to continuous labour of an unexciting kind. Yet all real civilization is at this price; without such labour, neither can the mind be disciplined into the habits required by a civilized society, nor the material world be prepared to receive it." Ibid., p. 265.

1

CIVILIZATION

NOTIONS OF A CULTURAL spectrum appeared early in the West and almost invariably entailed value judgements. The Greeks knew that they were Greeks, but that there were also "barbarians." The Romans knew that they were Romans, but also that those who inhabited the forests were "savages." The adjective "civilized," related both to the transformation of criminal into civil law and, more generally, to civility, made a later appearance. Rousseau had no difficulty in contrasting the civilized condition with noble savagery in his *Discours sur les sciences et arts* (1750), but he lacked the noun for what he so fiercely castigated. However, several decades later, in 1792, the French Foreign Minister named his daughter Civilization-Jémappes-République. Civilization had arrived in the intervening years as a highly value-charged term. Much the same happened in England. Despite Boswell's urging, Dr. Johnson, in 1772, denied the neologism entry into his dictionary. Yet, Johnson himself, had used the word two years before in a wholly admirable way: "a decent provision for the poor is the true test of civilization."[1] Perhaps the rejection had something to do with the good doctor's distaste for the Scots, whose theorists had already worked out an impressive scheme of social development from a primitive or "rude" state to a "civilized" state which, however, they were just as likely to call "polished" or "refined." Adam Smith drew upon the labours of these predecessors in *The Wealth of Nations* (1776), a work credited by the linguist, Beneviste, with much furthering the use of the term.[2] In fact, Smith made little use of the word itself, though his great book did encourage the spread of the idea that while there could exist other civilizations, like those of the ancient Egyptians or the contemporary Indians and Chinese, their distinguishing feature was stagnation.[3] Still inclined to think more in terms of "refinement" than of "civilization," another Scot, John Millar, argued that the level of development of a society could be gauged by the treatment of its women.[4]

Well launched by the end of the century, the notion of civilization was never without critics.[5] But by the 1820s, it had achieved such a hegemonic status that people as different as Metternich and Hugo tried to buttress their political and aesthetic positions with accounts of its development. But by the late nineteenth century, what had once been new coinage had become badly shopworn, an item of cant, invoked frequently but with scant attention paid to its possible meanings. By 1883, Sir John Seeley could describe "this theory of civilization" as "a very fair example of bad philosophizing."[6] Whatever the appeal of the Englishman's call for a more politically-focused history, the Western idea of civilization was more vulnerable to those dissatisfied with modernity: that is, from primitivists who rejected its complexity and artificiality; from theosophists and others who turned to "the wisdom of the East"; from aesthetes who preferred to identify with the "decadent" phases of past civilizations; and from those like Brooks and Henry past civilizations; and from those like Brooks and Henry Adams who worried about the decadence of their own civilization. But this cultural onslaught did not seriously harm the regard in which civilization continued to be held by those sectors of society who considered themselves respectable and refined.

It took World War I to pose the mortal threat. Figures as diverse as Henry James and Sigmund Freud recognized the danger almost immediately. The murderous prolongation of the struggle drove the point home to others. Those who clung to older notions of civilization in the immediate wake of the war could only appear ludicrous. If in 1919, *Figaro* announced the founding of an "International Federation of Europe and the world under the aegis of France, the guardian of civilization," in the same year Paul Valéry announced: "We later civilizations...we too now know that we are mortal."[7] If in the following year, the birth control advocate, Marie Stopes, managed to reduce the crisis of civilization to the servant problem, Ezra Pound was savage in his lament for the death of "a myriad" on behalf of "an old bitch gone in the teeth...a botched civilization."[8] There were, of course, more serious efforts at rehabilitation of the concept. Bloomsbury had its say in 1928 when Clive Bell championed the refinement of manners, the standards of taste, the sweep of toleration, and the leisure which he took to be intrinsic to civilization. But he gave the game away with the lament that "there are not now but two or three restaurants in London where it is an unqualified pleasure to dine."[9] Obviously, if civilization was to be vindicated, something much more tough-minded was in order. Two years later Freud supplied it in *Das Unbehagen in der Kultur*, translated into English as *Civilization and Its Discontents*.

Translating "Kultur" as "Civilization" was hardly unusual: Jacob Burckhardt's great work, for instance, had appeared in English as *The Civilization of the Renaissance*. But something far

3

more serious was involved in this case, for in 1927 Freud had declared bluntly: "I scorn to distinguish between culture and civilization."[10] He thus intervened directly in Central European cultural politics, with the works of two of his contemporaries, which appeared in the immediate wake of World War I, illustrating the nature of those politics. Thomas Mann argued in *Betrachtungen eines Unpolitischen*: "The difference between intellect and politics includes that of culture and civilization, of soul and society, of freedom and voting rights, of art, and literature; and German tradition is culture, soul, freedom, art and not civilization, society, voting rights and literature."[11] In *Der Untergang des Abendslandes*, Oswald Spengler differentiated between Culture, "living body of a soul…life in fullness and sureness of itself, formed by a growth from within," and Civilization, "the mummy," the "artificial, rootless life of our great cities, under forms fashioned by the intellect."[12]

Whatever the idiosyncracies of Mann's and Spengler's perspectives, in drawing a line between *Kultur* and *Zivilisation* to the detriment of the latter, they both indulged in a Central European truism which had originated in the late eighteenth century when German intellectuals had rebelled culturally against French-speaking courts. Compensating for their political impotence, they drew a distinction between the artificial *Zivilisation* characteristic of the princes and their courtiers and the more natural and moral *Kultur* possessed by themselves. Although the distinction received Kant's weighty imprimatur, it took the French and Industrial Revolutions, as well as the Romantic reaction to them, to consolidate fully the antithesis.

A more natural but also more spiritual, a more rooted and more Volkish *Kultur* came to be exalted at the expense of the artificial, mechanical, rootless and cosmopolitan *Zivilisation* supposedly characteristic of Western Europe. Neither enamoured of civilization like the French, nor confused about it like the English and Americans, the Central Europeans, when they considered it at all, settled for criticism of it.

Carried to its logical conclusion, this attitude threatened the massive industrialization begun in Germany in the last decades of the nineteenth century. Not surprisingly then, in 1897, the economist Werner Sombart warned the *Verein für Sozialpolitik*: "We must accept those...forms of economic life that are the most efficient, and for the rest we can be as moral as we like. But to be moral at the expense of economic progress is the beginning of the end of civilization."[13]

But such defences of the working of capitalism could not prevent its wrenching social consequences, and under the impact of these effects, the *Kultur-Zivilisation* antithesis had assumed more sinister features. Not only did the city and its proletariat come to represent civilization, but the Jew, portrayed as urban, rootless, materialistic, calculating and parasitic, came to be contrasted with the natural, rooted, spiritual, feeling and creative German. Freud, in brief, knew what he was doing when he scorned the antithesis.

The strength of the Germanic reaction to civilization reflected its initial identification with France where, having appeared under the *ancien régime*, the concept proved highly adaptable to the bourgeois order established by the Revolution. Outlining a developmental scheme in which his own era preceded that of human perfection, a victim of the Revolution, the Marquis de Condorcet, summed up the Enlightenment's idea of civilization:

> Manners have become less violent through the weakening of the prejudices that had maintained their savagery, through the influence of the spirit of industry and commerce which is inimical to unrest and violence as the natural enemies of wealth,

distant picture of the barbarism of the preceding stage, through a wider diffusion of the philosophical ideas of equality and humanity and, finally, through the influence, slow but sure, of the general progress of humanity.[14]

Benevolently expansive when it came to providing such blessings to those who lacked them, Condorcet sounded a note which would be repeated, sometimes with more cynicism, throughout the nineteenth century and beyond it. But less attention was paid to his call for "the complete annihilation of the prejudices which have brought about an inequality between the sexes."[15]

If Condorcet provided a progressive interpretation of the development of civilization, what is striking is the speed with which both supporters and opponents of the Revolution rallied to the idea of civilization. Stripped of much of Condorcet's optimism by the unfolding of the Revolution, the liberal Benjamin Constant still used the idea as the measure by which to condemn Bonapartist tyranny. But the idea also lent itself to use by conservatives and reactionaries. Thus, early in the nineteenth century, Chateaubriand and de Maistre could identify civilization with the papacy. But invocation was not exposition, and in the latter area Auguste Comte and François Guizot proved themselves especially influential in taking up Condorcet's task.

Comte argued in 1822, in terms which might well have been approved by the earlier Condorcet, that "the cultivated portion of the human race...has made uninterrupted progress in civilization from the most remote periods of history to our day."[16] Civilization, in his view, consisted "on the one hand in the development of the human mind, on the other in the result of this—namely the increasing power of man over nature. In other words, the component elements of civilization are education, the fine arts and industry."[17] Later he would complicate matters by maintaining that "the influence of civilization in perpetually improving the intellectual faculties is even more unquestionable than its effect on moral relations."[18] Eminently defensible in itself, this proposition received a peculiar twist because of his conviction of the intellectual superiority of the male and the moral superiority of the female. Comte, in other words, struck a note which would be echoed by positivists and non-positivists alike: women were, somehow or other, a moralizing and, hence, civilizing force, but were incapable of reaching the intellectual heights of civilization.

Paying scant attention to women, Guizot lectured in 1828 on "The History of Civilization in Europe" and in 1829 on "The History of Civilization in France." He presented civilization as "a fact like any other—a fact susceptible...of being studied, described and narrated."[19] With this "fact" at least potentially a "universal fact," he detected "a general destiny of humanity, a transmission of the aggregate of civilization; and, consequently, a universal history of civilization to be written."[20] Progress had to be central to such a history, and, though willing to recognize the existence of other civilizations, Guizot found them lacking in it. From his perspective, with France leading the way, only European civilization had progressed "according to the intentions of God."[21]

Other French historians shared Guizot's concerns. Although allowing for the contributions of other nations, Edgar Quinet claimed for France a special "instinct of civilization, the need to take the initiative in a general way to bring about progress in modern society."[22] Adolphe Thiers concluded characteristically that, without private property, "there can be no civilization."[23] Confronted in 1835 with industrial Manchester, Alexis de Tocqueville became almost dialectical: "Here humanity attains its most complete development and its most

7

humanity attains its most complete development and its most brutish; here civilization works its miracles, and civilized man is turned back almost into a savage."[24] Unable to settle for such contradictions, Jules Michelet exploded a decade later: "Today the rise and progress of the people are often compared to the invasion of the Barbarians. I like the word and accept the term. Barbarian! That is to say, full of new, vital, and regenerating vigor."[25] Such a position was easy enough for a quasi-Viconian to take, for presumably the new barbarism would be on a higher level than the old. In any event, as he aged, Michelet abandoned his identification with barbarism. Other revisions of youthful views also occurred. For instance, when he wrote *L'Avenir de la Science* in the heady days of 1848, Ernst Renan projected a democratic civilization which would be extended, albeit slowly, throughout the world. But when the tract finally appeared in 1890, the "Preface" proclaimed bluntly: "The idea of egalitarian civilization...is...a dream. The inequality of races is established."[26]

The racist interpretation of civilization had been most systematically developed by Arthur de Gobineau in his *Essai sur l'inégalité des races humaines* (1853-1855). Scornfully dismissing the liberal arguments of Guizot, he elaborated in ponderous detail a scheme in which racial mixture worked to produce civilization before excessive mixture brought on decay. Often misinterpreted, especially by his German followers, his message hardly was conducive to solace. He spent an entire chapter explaining that "our civilization is not superior to those which existed before it."[27] But he had no doubt about the superiority of those civilizations in which the Aryan element had predominated. The problem, for Gobineau, was that such was no longer the case in his own world where "the decaying march to decrepitude" had begun.[28] Significantly, the second edition of Gobineau's book sold better in the 1880s than the first had in the 1850s.

The Franco-Prussian War and the Commune separated the two editions. While it was easy enough to denounce Prussians and Communards as barbarians and savages, both events still raised agonizing questions about the much-vaunted French civilization. Most strikingly, notions of decadence, largely confined to psychiatric and literary circles under the Second Empire, began to command wider attention. Théophile Funck-Brentano tried to confront the new questions in *La Civilisation et ses lois morales sociales* (1876). While warning that "the emancipation of women" would destroy "the last support of civilization," he displayed more originality in arguing that civilization secreted within itself the forces which threatened it:

> ...the instincts are refined and needs are multiplied, thought is developed and divided to infinity; the social constitution becomes complicated, accord between his thoughts and his acts is more difficult for every man; the difference grows in the relations of people with each other, within a single people, and in the relations of peoples with each other.[29]

Civilization, in such circumstances, could all too easily turn into barbarism. Calling for moral and intellectual reform, especially on the part of the ruling class, Funck-Brentano left the possibility of renewal an open question.

The following decades supplied diverse answers. Warnings and calls for renewal continued. Thus, the philosopher Charles Renouvier lamented in 1896: "People will not realize the danger that civilization is running by the reluctance of the governing classes to enter upon a bold programme of social reform."[30] But for some, decadence became not a threat, but a delight. As the poet Verlaine put it, "I like the word decadence...it suggests the refined thoughts of extreme civilization, a high literary culture, a soul capable of intense pleasure."[31] Yet, despite the crisis of confidence triggered by the Franco-Prussian War and the Commune, a much more distinctly bourgeois sense of civilization reasserted itself in the Third Republic, whose primary school textbooks presented even the Gauls as the antitheses of ideally thoroughly civilized citizens. Quite characteristically, arguing for the holding of an international exposition in 1900, a deputy proclaimed in the Chambre: "France owes it to herself as the Queen of Civilization to hold a great exhibition."[32]

Nowhere was the confidence in civilization asserted more forcefully than in regard to the colonial sphere. In 1765, in one of the first uses of the term, the Abbé Baudeau asserted, with regard to the Amerindians of France's small Latin American holdings, that it was necessary "to convert them not only to the Christian faith, but also to European civilization."[33] If at the height of the Revolution Condorcet had projected the extension of the benefits of enlightened civilization to non-Western peoples, in 1849 Victor Hugo's journal provided its own gloss on that message in arguing for the acquisition of Madagascar:

> France is composing a poem that has for its title the conquest of Africa...She resorts to war...only to the extent that it is necessary for civilization. What reassures her is that she knows she bears in her hand light and liberty; she knows that, for a savage people to be occupied by France is to begin to be free, for a city of barbarians, to be burned by France is to begin to be enlightened.[34]

A speaker at a colonial banquet in 1906 drew upon decades of rhetoric when he proclaimed:

France has not wanted to see in the creation of her colonies a simple extension of political domination, still less of her commercial exploitation. She has seen a means of making penetrate, among the peoples outside the general movement of civilization, those of her ideas which have place her at the head of the civilization of the world.[35]

However brutal its actual implementation, the *mission civilisatrice* had genuine appeal, for it both facilitated exploitation and eased consciences.

Although taken seriously enough by some, France's famed *mission civilisatrice* served as a mantle capacious enough to excuse industrial and commercial backwardness vis-à-vis Great Britain, and to disguise somewhat the often conflicting and sometimes sordid interests behind French imperialism. But it did pose problems on occasion. A revealing exchange took place in the Chambre on July 28, 1885. The expansionist, Jules Ferry, summarized, fairly enough, the arguments of his anti-imperialist opponent, Camille Pelletan: "What sort of civilization is this which is imposed by gun-fire? Is it anything more than a form of barbarism?"[36] Characterizing such questions as "political metaphysics," a deadly enough slur under the positivist Republic, Ferry insisted upon the "duty" of "superior races...to civilize the inferior races."[37] But his introduction of racial rankings into the debate had to do with cultural rather than biological differences. For "assimilationist" imperialists like himself, the *mission civilisatrice* turned, in theory at least, on the extension of the benefits of civilization, by force if necessary, to peoples deemed capable of reaching, or almost reaching, the heights scaled previously by the French themselves. By the late nineteenth century, however, this perspective was being challenged by "associationists" like Leopold de Saussure who argued: "All mature societies are capable of

11

progress, but they are not capable of progress identical to that of France, for two different societies of different races cannot follow the same path of development."[38]

If neither imperial policy nor conditions in the colonies ever approached the ideals sketched by colonial theorists in the comfort of Paris, imperialism, including that of France, did contribute to the outbreak of World War I. While French propagandists presented the struggle as one between progressive civilization and barbarous militarism, the ongoing carnage inevitably raised some profound doubts about much-lauded civilization. As Louis Mairet reflected in 1916: "Confronted by the spectacle of a scientific struggle in which Progress is used to return to Barbarism and by the spectacle of a civilization turning against itself to destroy itself, reason cannot cope."[39] Accompanied by horrors which he could not have imagined in the 1870s, Funck-Brentano's vision of an implosion of civilization was coming to be realized. Civilization now seemed to carry within itself the seeds of its own destruction. Victory only partially assuaged the doubts of those like Valéry who had learned of the mortality of their civilizations. Ritualistic invocations of the old ideal could only rouse the derision of the cultural *avant-garde*, made up of the Surrealists and others, but, more significantly, could not dispel the malaise which stalked France during the inter-war period. Too many had experienced the murderous effects of barbed wire, machine guns and heavy artillery. Industrial civilization, so often celebrated at the International Expositions, had revealed itself as technologically refined barbarism.

If the notion of civilization was also severely tested in England by World War I, it had never taken as firm a hold there as in France. Almost from the time of the appearance of the notion, a certain degree of confusion characterized English approaches to it. If some readily accepted civilization, others subscribed to the civilization-culture distinction, and yet others used the two categories inter-changeably. The confusion stimulated serious efforts to clarify the nature of civilization. These diverse efforts, however, did not end in consensus or, for that matter, even much clarity. The Americans, who followed the English lead in this respect, were consequently left oscillating between self-doubt and assertiveness.

Although the definition of civilization as a refinement of manners had an obvious appeal to an ascending class, the English middle class also managed to find in it values more immediately congenial. Thomas Malthus solemnly intoned in the second edition of his *Essay on Population* (1803): "To the laws and property and marriage, and to the narrow principle of self-interest...we are indebted for all the noble exertions of human genius, for everything which distinguishes the civilized from the savage state."[40] A staunch believer in Malthus' ideas in regard to population, James Mill adapted the notion of civilization to the utilitarian concerns which he shared with his friend Bentham: "Exactly in proportion as *Utility* is the object of every pursuit, we may regard a nation as civilized."[41] The utilitarian emphasis would eventually lead to the argument that the use of the bodies of the poor for medical research would be "a step in civilization."[42]

One did not, however, have to go so far in pursuit of the middle-class millennium. In *The Moral and Physical Condition of the Working Classes Employed in the Cotton Manufactures in Manchester* (1832), James P. Shuttleworth maintained that "a system which promotes the advance of civilization, and diffuses it all over the world—which promises to maintain the peace of nations, by establishing a permanent international law, founded on the benefits of commercial association, cannot be inconsistent with the happiness of the great mass of people."[43] Six years later, Richard Cobden reinforced the message: "Commerce is the great panacea which, like a beneficial medical discovery, will serve to inoculate with the healthy and saving taste for civilization all the nations of the world."[44] Although this kind of thinking would echo throughout the nineteenth century and beyond, it reached its apotheosis at the 1851 Exhibition when Albert, Prince Consort, proclaimed: *"the great principle of division of labour*, which may be called the moving power of civilization, is being extended to all branches of science, industry and art."[45]

Despite this august endorsement, civilization's links with industry and commerce, economic liberalism and utilitarianism, had already roused unease on the part of some. In 1818, Coleridge introduced a distinction between "civilization" and "cultivation" and, in another essay of the same year, echoed Kant in describing "Young men...perilously over-civilized, and most pitiably uncultivated."[46] In *On the Constitution of Church and State* (1830), he warned:

> But civilization is itself but a mixed good, if not far more a corrupting influence...and a nation so distinguished more fitly to be called a varnished rather than a polished people; where this civilization is not grounded in *cultivation*, in the harmonious development of those qualities and faculties that characterize our humanity.[47]

Yet, in the English fashion of the *via media*, Coleridge rather fancied having his cake and eating it too. Redefining the National Church and broadening its clergy into a "clerisy," he assigned the Church and its agents "the progressive civilization of the community."[48] In this process the mass of the population would be brought to comprehend "the permanent *distinction*, and the occasional *contrast*, between cultivation and civilization...to understand this most valuable lesson taught by history...that a nation can never be too cultivated, but may easily become an over-civilized race."[49]

Buffeted by the ideas of Bentham and Coleridge and perhaps more aware than any other Englishman of his day of the
work of the French historians, John Stuart Mill took up the
problem in 1838. He drew a line, not between culture and
civilization, but between two different meanings of civilization, the first of which involved *"human improvement* in
general," the second, *"certain kinds* of improvement in particular."[50] Focusing on the second, he struck a modified
Coleridgean note: "we hold that civilization is good, that it is
the cause of much good and is not incompatible with any; but
we think there is other good, much even of the highest good,
which civilization in this sense does not provide for, and some
of which it has a tendency...to impede."[51] Taken in this second
sense, he acknowledged the benefits of greater security of person and property, as well as a greater diffusion of knowledge,
but the future author of *On Liberty* (1859) already worried that
"by the natural growth of civilization...the weight and importance of the individual, as compared with the mass, sinks into
greater and greater insignificance."[52] Yet, for all his worries
about the threat to the individual posed by civilization, Mill
did not doubt its intrinsic worth for those capable of receiving
it. But for the moment that did not include everybody, least of
all those peoples whose condition approached the bestial.

Although the 1838 essay provided his most extended discussion of civilization, this was neither the first nor the last
time that Mill confronted the issue. In 1826 he had invoked the
authority of John Millar, "perhaps the greatest of the
philosophical inquirers into civilization," in arguing that
"good treatment of women...is one of the surest marks of high
civilization."[53] With feminism perhaps the most constant and
consistent conviction of his life, Mill was more at fault in ignoring a caution which appeared in his *Logic* (1843): "the word (as
Civilization, for example) which professes to be designating
the unknown common property, conveys to scarcely any

minds the same idea."[54] If his own usage of the term could be loose, he made startlingly clear the hopes he held out for it: "Civilization in every one of its aspects is a struggle against the animal instincts. Over some of the strongest of them, it has shown itself capable of acquiring abundant control. It has artificialized large portions of mankind to such an extent, that of their most natural inclinations they have scarce a vestige of remembrance....If it has not brought the instinct of population under as much restraint as is needful, we must remember that it has never been seriously tried."[55]

While entertaining such hopes, Mill remained none too clear about the contents of civilization. A non-Coleridgean conservative, in fact, had considerable less difficulty with it. Presented in *On the Scope and Nature of a University Education* (1853), John Henry Newman's claims on behalf of his own civilization, measured even by the standards of the times, outdid those of any Philosophical Radical or member of the Manchester School:

> ...though there are other civilizations in the world... yet this civilization, together with the society which is its creation and home, is so distinctive and luminous in its character, so imperial in its extent, so imposing in its duration, and so utterly without rival upon the face of the earth, that the association may fully assume to itself the title of 'human society', and its civilization the abstract term 'civilization'.[56]

Untempted by the culture-civilization distinction, the Catholic cleric designated this commonwealth: "preeminently and emphatically human society, and its intellect the human mind, and its decisions the sense of mankind, its disciplined and cultivated state civilization in the abstract, and the territory on which its lies the *orbis terrarum*, or the world."[57] While many other Westerners believed all of that, few possessed Newman's ability to garb their belief in such majestic language.

Measured against such stately prose, Matthew Arnold's *Culture & Anarchy* (1859) comes close to being the work of one of those Philistines who, along with the Barbarians and Populace, he considered the constituents of the majority within English society. Returning to a Coleridgean perspective, Arnold went beyond the earlier Germanophile in sharpening the culture-civilization antithesis:

> Above all in our country has culture a weighty part to perform, because here that mechanical character, which civilization tends to take everywhere, is shown to the most eminent degree...the idea of perfection as an *inward* condition of the mind and spirit is at variance with the mechanical and material civilization in esteem with us, and nowhere...so much as in esteem with us.[58]

His ideal lay with a culture which "places human perfection in an internal condition, in the growth and preponderance of our humanity proper, as distinguished from our animality."[59]

Arnold treated civilization more favourably elsewhere. He began his essay on "Equality" with an apparent paradox: Sir Erskine May, after describing the damage done to France by notions of social equality, still had to admit: "Yet is she high, if not the first in the scale of civilized nations."[60] Arnold found no paradox. Charging May with having failed to define civilization, he proffered his own definition: "Civilization is the humanization of man in society."[61] Hence, "to be the most civilized of nations...is to be the nation which comes nearest to human perfection."[62] Culture, in brief, had been transformed into civilization. The contempt for the Philistine, however, remained:

Your middle-class man thinks it is the highest pitch of development and civilization when his letters are carried twelve times a day from Islington to Camberwell, and from Camberwell to Islington, and if railway trains run to and from between them every quarter of an hour.[63]

From Arnold's perspective, the railway might possibly be an instrument of civilization, but, in and of itself, it could not serve as a symbol, let alone the symbol, of civilization.

If philosophers like Mill, theologians like Newman, and men of letters like Arnold took civilization seriously, the historians, despite Seeley's complaints, largely ignored the matter. Henry Thomas Buckle's *History of Civilization in England* (1856-1861) was the sole work which approached the level achieved by the French in this regard. A radical and a positivist, Buckle acknowledged the existence of other civilizations in the present, only to draw a distinction between "the tendency in Europe...to subordinate nature to men; out of Europe to subordinate men to nature."[64] As he presented the matter, "national progress in connection with popular liberty, could have originated in no part of the world but in Europe; where, therefore, real civilization and the encroachments of the human mind upon the forces of nature, are alone to be studied."[65]

If the English lagged behind the French in history, they took the lead in cultural anthropology, possibly as a result of the diversion of the French into an often racist physical anthropology. Yet an ambiguity stalked this anthropology. E.B. Tylor began *The Origins of Culture* (1872) by defining "Civilization or Culture" as "that complex whole which includes knowledge, belief, art, morals, laws, customs, and any other capabilities and habits acquired by man as a member of society."[66] Tylor, like Arnold in the end, conflated culture and civilization. Sharing the proclivity of his contemporaries to establish a scale of civilization on the basis of material, intellectual, moral and other capabilities, he adopted the evolutionary perspective:

> From an ideal point of view, civilization may be looked upon as a general improvement of mankind by higher organization of individual and society, to the end of promoting at once man's goodness, power and happiness. This theoretical civilization does in no small measure correspond to actual civilization, as traced by comparing savagery with barbarism, and barbarism with modern educated life.[67]

While he recognized some difficulties with the political and moral dimensions of the scale, he insisted

> ...that any known savage would not be improved by judicious civilization, is a proposition which no moralist would dare to make; when the general tenor of the evidence goes far to justify the view that on the whole the civilized man is not only wiser and more capable than the savage, but also better and happier, and that the barbarian stands between.[68]

Civilization, in brief, promised to ameliorate the condition of and increase the happiness of the savages existing both abroad and at home.

Darwin acknowledged his debts to Tylor and other anthropologists in *The Descent of Man* (1871): notions of biological and social evolution mutually reinforced each other. Darwin himself, both painstaking and daring in his scientific work, remained otherwise very much the conventional Victorian. He believed that private property, the division of labour, and the formation of social ranks or classes gave rise to civilization and, not least, to the development of the moral qualities associated with it. But he also found that it posed a major biological problem: "civilization...checks in many ways the action of natural selection."[69] In his view, the very moral qualities which had developed with civilization and testified to its worth inhibited the ruthlessness intrinsic to natural selection and increased the importance of sexual selection. Driven to confronting human sexuality in its most immediate form, the great biologist, most uncharacteristically but very revealingly, fell back upon Schopenhauer who had observed that "the final end of all love intrigues, be they tragic or comic, is really of more importance than all the ends of human life. What it all turns on is nothing less than the composition of the next generation."[70]

Schopenhauer, of course, was no friend to women, and, though much more the gentleman, neither was Darwin. With no sense of the historical conditions which might have accounted for the results, he ran through what had become the standard exercise of calling for lists of men and women who had distinguished themselves in a variety of fields and allowed, at best, that "with woman the powers of intuition, of rapid perception, and perhaps of imitation, are more strongly marked than in man."[71] He added immediately: "some, at least, of these faculties are characteristic of the lower races and therefore of a past and lower state of civilization."[72] Darwin's scientific genius would lend his extra-scientific pronouncements an aura which would be seized upon by misogynists, imperialists, and eugenicists. But what they found in Darwin was hardly original. There was, in fact, Social Darwinism before there was Darwin.

Having been in a convoluted fashion an agent of British expansionism aboard the *Beagle*, the great scientist's ideas, including those having to do with civilization, could be invoked to justify British imperialism. But with the British, civilization never assumed the importance that it did with the French. Possessed of a much stronger industrial base, they had less cause to call upon this disputed notion in support of their overseas activities. For ideological purposes, moreover, the rich store of Protestant rhetoric allowed them to cast their "mission" in terms of "evangelizing" rather than "civilizing," though the two were often enough yoked together. More fundamentally, the British had no French Revolution to make good upon or for which to apologize.

Despite pronouncements like Macaulay's Indian Education Minute of 1835, assimilationist tendencies were curbed by either explicitly racist or more vaguely cultural assumptions of superiority to those whom they ruled or hoped to rule. Consequently, though civilization was never reduced to a side-show, it remained one talisman among others. The explorer Richard Burton observed:

> Whenever good Madame Britannia is about to break the eighth commandment, she simultaneously displays a lot of piety, much rhapsodizing about the bright dawn of Christianity, the finger of Providence, the spread of civilization, and the infinite benefits conveyed upon the barbarians by permitting them to become her subjects, to pay their rent to her.[73]

The explorer knew something about such matters.

Despite the variety of existing justifications for expansion, British imperialists welcomed Darwin's views on the matter. Walter Bagehot drew upon them in his somewhat mistitled *Physics and Politics* (1872), but introduced nuances of his own. Arguing that "a stationary state is by far the most frequent condition of man...the progressive state is only a rare and occasional exception," he posited several kinds of arrested development, with the extreme case being that of the Australian aborigines, the usual victims of the obsession with civilization.[74] Having tried to temper Darwinism with Christianity in *Social Evolution* (1894), Benjamin Kidd turned to more materialistic considerations in *The Control of the Tropics* (1898) where he argued that those regions "be governed as a trust for civilization."[75] He then attempted to buttress such claims in the turgid *Principles of Western Civilization* (1902) where he asserted the primacy of the West.

While certainly true in material terms, that primacy was already being questioned. The concern with decadence was not solely a French obsession. The Conservative Alfred Balfour, in the wake of the Boer War, felt impelled to address the issue directly in *Decadence* (1908). After repeating a series of what had once been Liberal verities, he announced that he had failed to find any "symptom either of pause or of regression in the onward movement which for more than a thousand years had been characteristic of Western civilization."[76] The following year the Liberal C.F.G. Masterman struck a more pessimistic note:

> The large hopes and dreams of Early Victorian times have vanished.... Civilization, in the early twentieth century in England, suffers no illusions as to the control of natural forces, or the exploitation of natural secrets furnishing a cure either for the diseases from which it suffers in the body, or the more deeply seated malaise of the soul.[77]

Clearly, Liberal and Conservative positions had been exchanged.

Nevertheless, in bringing Great Britain into World War I, the Liberal prime minister, Asquith, invoked the principles of civilization. Thus, Clive Bell began his later discussion of civilization at the right place: "Since from August 1914 to November 1918 Great Britain and her Allies were fighting for civilization, it cannot be impertinent to enquire what civilization may be."[78] Having confessed an inability to provide a precise definition of the term, he fell back upon a series of Bloomsbury platitudes. Yet, in the face of the casualties inflicted by the war, bafflement in the face of civilization was understandable enough. Only the belligerents least touched by the war, the Americans, emerged from it with their confidence in civilization heightened. Participation in the war, entailing both the display of power and closer acquaintance with Europeans, seems to have freed them from those insecurities which in the nineteenth century had only been partially masked by an aggressive self-assertiveness.

During that century, the Americans, like the English, had brought together Christianity, commerce and industry, and Anglo-Saxon racism as the accompaniments or defining qualities of civilization. Unlike the English, however, they had a frontier close at hand. Whereas the English could afford to place peoples encountered overseas on a scale of temporal evolution, the Americans confronted both time and space in their discussions of the relationship between savagery and civilization. A very shrewd commentator, Thomas Jefferson, put the matter well in 1824:

> Let a philosophic observer commence a journey from the savages of the Rocky Mountains, eastwards toward the sea-coast. Those he would observe in the earliest stages of association living under no law but that of nature, subsisting and covering themselves with the flesh and skins of wild beasts. He would next find those on our frontiers in the pastoral state, raising domestic animals to supply the defects of hunting. Then succeed our own semi-civilized citizens, the

pioneers of the advance of civilization, and so in his progress, he would meet the gradual shades of improving man until he would reach his, as yet most improved state in the seaport towns. This, in fact, is equivalent to a survey, in time, of the progress of man from the infancy of creation to the present day.[79]

The notion of civilization, in the American case, was explosively expansive from even before the appearance of the word. The nineteenth century brought the drive to full swell. With his eyes fixed on Oregon, Joseph Richardson told Congress in 1828 that Americans had been "destined by Providence to carry westward...the blessings of civilization and liberty."[80] Calling for the annexation of Mexico in 1847, the *Baltimore Sun* promised the improvement of conditions through "the steamboat, the railroad, the telegraph, and above all the schoolhouse, with various minor instrumentalities of a refined and enlightened civilization."[81] Urging the absorption of Mexico, Latin America and Canada in *The American Republic* (1860), Orestes Brownsen doubted they would be missed as political entities, for "the work of civilization could go on without them."[82] As for the acquisition of the Philippines at the end of the century, Senator Albert A. Beveridge proclaimed that Americans would "not renounce our part in the mission of our race, trustee under God, of the civilization of the world."[83] At a somewhat less lofty level, the "Admiral Dewey" issue of *Harper's Weekly*, from its start a "journal of civilization," carried the following advertisement: "The first step towards lightening THE WHITE MAN'S BURDEN is through teaching the virtues of cleanliness. PEAR'S SOAP is a potent factor in brightening the dark corners of the globe as civilization advances."[84]

Such sentiments received full expression in Josiah Strong's *Our Country: Its Possible Future and the Present Crisis* (1886) in which the apocalyptic and the eschatological mingled. Although he worried about a variety of domestic evils, Strong believed the Anglo-Saxon race destined "to give civilization to mankind."[85] He was equally sure that the centre of the coming global civilization would be the United States. In support of that proposition, he drew upon the theories of Dr. George Beard who had outlined a link between his psychiatric notion of "neurasthenia" and civilization in order to argue that the Americans, with the most neurasthenics in their population, constituted the vanguard of civilization. Strong asserted:

> The roots of civilization are the nerves; and other things being equal, the finest nervous organization will produce the highest civilization....The physical changes, accompanied by the mental, which are taking place in the people of the United States are apparently to adapt man to the demands of a higher civilization.[86]

Strong's arguments would amuse Matthew Arnold.

Not all Americans were so willing to celebrate the virtues, nervous and otherwise, of their civilization. In a work which was initially to be entitled "anti-Cant," *The American Democrat* (1838), James Fenimore Cooper found his fellows all too insufficiently civilized. In this fierce polemic against Jacksonian democracy, he insisted on the necessity for civilization of private property, social and sexual hierarchy, good food and manners, and especially individualism before concluding that, in these respects, Americans had regressed since the founding of the republic only a half century earlier. The affronted Cooper, in brief, failed to achieve the calm and confidence of the Transcendental sage of Cambridge, Ralph Waldo Emerson.

Having lectured on culture in 1837, Emerson later turned his attention to civilization. He began the essay devoted to it with a poem in which he refused to "count the Sioux a match for Agassiz."[87] But if the frontier could not be escaped even in placid Cambridge, Emerson set his mind on loftier matters. Acknowledging that civilization was "a vague, complex name of many degrees," he alleged that "nobody has attempted a definition," by which he presumably meant that nobody had provided a definition satisfactory enough to be commonly accepted.[88] Undeterred by such failures, he defined it as "learning the secret of cumulative power" which, in turn, implied "a faculty of association, power to compare, the ceasing from fixed ideas."[89] Viewed from this perspective, the Chinese and Japanese were civilized, but black Africans and Amerindians were not. Yet even the former were not wholly civilized. Numbering among civilization's features agriculture, the division of labour, industry, markets, the post-office, newspapers and a right regard for women, Emerson concluded that "the true test of civilization is…the kind of man the country turns out."[90]

Decades later two other New Englanders, Brooks and Henry Adams, took a more morose view of the matter. In 1895, Brooks Adams published *The Law of Civilization and Decay*, a proto-Spenglarian exercise focused on the contrast between dispersion (barbarism) and concentration (civilization). Early in the new century, his brother composed *The Education of Henry Adams*. Turning back to Gibbon on the steps of Santa Maria di Ara Caeli, but in a mood vastly different from that of his greater predecessor, he acknowledged the Roman Empire and the Catholic Church as the "two great experiments of Western civilization" and wondered whether Rome "might still survive to express the failure of a third."[91] If the Adams brothers could be taken as living illustrations of the purported link between neurasthenia and civilization, Americans who interpreted the connection in an optimistic fashion would find their buoyancy confirmed early in the new century by the economist Simon Nelson Patten's discovery of the "new basis of civilization" in the consumer society: "The new morality does not consist in saving but in expanding consumption."[92]

Americans were likely to be especially defensive in the face of the critical comments of foreigners, and there was plenty of such. The greatest of the foreign commentators, Tocqueville, seemed to give with one hand and take away with the other: "The inhabitants of the United States constitute a great civilized people, which fortune has placed in an uncultivated country, at a distance of three thousand miles from the central point of civilization."[93] In his view, if the United States was the only country "where the continued right of association has been introduced into civil life and where all the advantages which civilization can confer are procured by means of it," it was also the case that "in few of the civilized nations of our times have the higher sciences made less progress…and in few have great artists, distinguished poets, or celebrated authors been more rare."[94] Lacking his compatriot's sense of balance, Comte dismissed "the childishly illusionary claims of political superiority where the essential elements proper to modern civilization are still so imperfectly developed, saving only industrial activity."[95] That very industrial activity, however, terrified the Goncourt brothers in 1867: "The Universal Exposition, the final blow levelled at the past, the Americanization of France, industry lording it over art, the steam thresher displacing the painting—in brief, the Federation of Matter."[96] French intellectuals would continue to perceive "Americanization" as a threat, if not *the* threat, to their civilization.

English observers were scarcely kinder. To take but a single case, Matthew Arnold attempted a nuanced appraisal in "Civilization in the United States" (1888). Now defining civilization as "the power of conduct, the power of intellect and knowledge, the power of social life and manners," he admitted that his view differed from that of most people who saw it as "a satisfaction, not of all the main demands of human nature, but of the demand for the comforts and conveniences of life."[97] He recognized that more Americans than Englishmen shared in the latter benefits and found that admirable enough, but he insisted on turning to "some other and better tests by which to try the civilization of the United States."[98] Those tests led to a brutal conclusion: "a great void exists in the civilization over there: a want of what is elevated and beautiful; of what is interesting."[99]

In their sensitivity to foreign criticism the Americans resembled the Russians, whose relationship to civilization was even more complex. Turgenev, who spent much of his life outside of Russia, declared firmly: "My faith is in civilization, and I require no further creed."[100] The sociologist, Peter Lavrov, produced an analysis which, while it reflected specifically Russian conditions, was perhaps more powerful than anything produced in Europe or the United States during the nineteenth century:

> Primitive human societies are held together by sacred bonds. These bonds constitute *culture*, which progressed towards *civilization* only through the operation of critical thought. The bearers of this thought make up the intelligentsia, membership in which is a high privilege capable of being repaid to society only through devotion to social ends.[101]

But members of that intelligentsia, not all of them Slavophiles, had their doubts about civilization or at least about Western civilization. Supremely civilized himself, Alexander Herzen projected a future in which "civilization will perish—will as Proudhon politely puts it, be *liquidated*."[102] The liberal Nikolai Ivanovich Nadezhdin maintained that "it is not our role to be an echo of a civilization which lies in ruins and agony and of which we see perhaps already the convulsions announcing its death, but to produce ourselves a new, young, strong civilization, a genuine Russian civilization which will renew old Europe."[103]

Sentiments like Nadezhdin's were often prompted by critical comments from abroad. The French favoured the Poles among the Slavs. Addressing the Chamber of Peers in 1846, Hugo proclaimed: "The French people has been civilization's missionary in Europe; the Polish people, its knight."[104] The other side of pro-Polish sentiment was Russophobia. Diderot had noted as early as 1780 in connection with Russia: "the *freeing*, or that which is the same thing, the *civilization* of an empire is a long and difficult work."[105] Resting upon more concrete information, this remained the message of the Marquis de Custine in *La Russie en 1839* (1839). A conservative who had expected to appreciate Czarist Russia, Custine had been bitterly disappointed. Believing that "civilization is not a fashion, nor an artificial device, it is a power which has a result," he did "not reproach the Russians for being what they are, what I blame in them is, their pretending to be what we are....Thus they are spoilt for the savage state, and yet wanting in the requisites of civilization."[106] His final judgement was brutal: "it is a barbarism plastered over, and nothing more."[107] Some perceived such barbarism as a vital threat to Europe itself. Thus, the historian, Henri Martin, warned in *La Russie et l'Europe* (1875), that unless Europe federated, it would be conquered by Russia, with the Americans being left to preserve "all the higher elements of human civilization."[108] Foreign relations, however, did not work out in the fashion projected by Martin. With the Franco-Russian alliance, French republicans welcomed Czarist Russians into Western civilization, and French literary circles toasted the glorious names of Dostoevsky and Tolstoy who, unfortunately, had little good to say about that civilization.

Engaged in "the great game" with Russia throughout the nineteenth century, the English paid more attention to power relations than to literary matters. But they did not overlook entirely Russia's claims to a civilizing mission of its own. Commenting in 1865 on opinion regarding Russia, Sir Henry Rawlinson noted:

> A considerable section of the community...believes... that the extension of Russian power in Central Asia is a consummation devoutly to be worked for. To substitute civilization—albeit not of the highest type—for the grovelling superstition, the cruelty, depravity, the universal misery which now prevails in Uzbeg and Afghan principalities, appears...an object of paramount importance, regarding the general interests of humanity.[109]

This Major-General's own views lay closer to those of his queen who, when faced in the 1870s with what she deemed Disraeli's weakness in dealing with the Russians, wrote to the prime minister: "She feels she cannot...remain the sovereign of a country that is letting itself down to kiss the feet of the great barbarians, the retarders of all liberty and civilization."[110]

Whatever the promising futures sometimes allotted to the United States and Russia, they were most often seen by Europe as marginal to civilization. Of much more importance was how Europeans judged each other in light of civilization. With the Germans largely removed from the quarrel because of their distinction between *Kultur* and *Zivilization*, it basically became a dispute between the French and the English. Fully prepared to accept the judgement of "all Europe" that France was "the most civilized of all its nations," Guizot was himself sufficiently civilized to consider the claims of others."[111] While he lauded the social achievements of the

English, he thought them to have been purchased at the expense of both the individual and humanity. Buckle, of course, did not see the matter in that fashion. He, too, ran through the claims of various European nations to the highest degree of civilization. Calling the French "a great and splendid people," he found them "unfit to exercise political power."[112] The introduction of this political criterion compelled this hard-headed positivist to put the liberal paradise, his own country, at civilization's summit.

That kind of argument, however, did not entirely assuage English unease in view of French claims of superiority. Attempting to still doubts, the journalist, George W. Stevens, announced in *Glimpses of Three Nations* (1901): "Our civilization is the kind we can pass on to the lower states of humanity, to their great benefit and our own. The Parisian civilization is a rare vintage that loses its bouquet the moment it passes outside the fortifications."[113] But others worried that the French vintage travelled all too well. Great Britain's pro-consul in Egypt, Lord Cromer, presented the Egyptian as placed between "a damsel possessing attractive, albeit somewhat artificial charms" and "a sober, elderly matron of perhaps somewhat greater moral worth, but less pleasing outward appearance."[114] As a man of the world, he understood the attraction of the former. As a servant of the empire, he thought that the better chances for character formation lay with the latter. In any event, the contemporary Egyptian had no case for autonomy, let alone independence: before that could happen "the new generation...has to be persuaded or forced into imbibing the true spirit of Western civilization."[115] If Islam hindered imbibing of any sort, this was especially true in regard to Western ideas in regard to women. In Islamic societies, like that of Egypt, "the position of women...is...a fatal obstacle to that elevation of thought and character which should accompany the introduction of European civilization."[116]

Behind the Egypt of Cromer's day loomed that of antiquity and, more generally, an aged and ageless Orient. Despite an Egyptianizing craze introduced by Bonaparte's expedition at the end of the eighteenth century, ancient Egypt would come to be condemned on three scores: association with Africa, with the Semites, and with the Orient. The last, the Orient, lent itself to a variety of interpretations. If romantics like Friedrich Schlegel gushed over it, what they had in mind was an Orient which was mummified and only to be revived through the imagination or, more mundanely, though philology. But the Orient could also be presented in terms of extreme civilization, a condition which might be admired, but which was more frequently abhorred. Writing to Tocqueville from Persia but also taking into account India and China, Gobineau remarked:

> To substitute beautiful manners for private and public
> morality, to permit cruelty as long as it is not accom-
> panied by marks of passion, to tolerate everything as
> long as all that is ignoble and even odious is cloaked
> by smiling and pleasant appearance—I confess that I
> see in this...the last word in what is called civiliza-
> tion.[117]

The fundamental charge brought against the Orient, however, was that it was stationary, that is, that it lacked the Western experience of progress. If Adam Smith played a major role in bringing together ancient Egypt, as well as the India and China of his day, in a persuasive depiction of stagnation, others soon followed his lead. The enlightened and gentle Condorcet maintained that "the human mind, given up to ignorance and prejudice, was condemned to shameful stagnation in those vast empires whose uninterrupted existence has dishonoured Asia for so long."[118] Linked to notions of "Oriental despotism" which went back to the Greeks, the stagnation-progress polarity provided the standard for judging the civilizations of India and China.

As part of his quarrel with the Sanskritist, Sir William Jones, James Mill asserted in *The History of British India* (1818): "The term civilization was by him, as with most men, attached to no fixed and definite assemblance of ideas."[119] Mill believed that, through the use of the utility principle as yardstick, "a scale of civilization can be found."[120] Not only did that scale exclude black Africans from civilization, but it also placed Hindu civilization below that of the roughly comparable Arabs, Persians and Chinese. India had failed to progress since the time of Alexander. Although he allowed for the wrenching changes introduced by British rule, Marx's opinion at mid-century was none too far from Mill's: "However changing the political aspect of India's past must appear, its social condition has remained unaltered from its remotest antiquity, until the first decennium of the nineteenth century."[121] Whatever the degree of change introduced by the British, its pace disappointed some. But that could be explained. Finding the greatest contrast between "the old eastern and customary civilizations and the new western and changeable civilization," Bagehot argued: "we are attempting...to pour what we can of a civilization whose spirit is progress into a civilization whose spirit is fixity."[122] So far the Indian experiment seemed to indicate that "a highly civilized race may fail in producing a rapidly excellent effect in a less civilized race, because it is too good and too different."[123]

The French traveller, Gustave Le Bon, picked up on the standard contrast:

> England is the Western world with its complex civilization developing itself according to a geometric progression and marching rapidly, on the basis of new

forces, towards an uncertain future. India is the East immobilized in an eternal dream, its eyes fixed not on the future but on the past, relentlessly probing the thought of its ancestors and its gods.[124]

Changes, some of them disturbing, were taking place. An associationist rather than an assimilationist in regard to his own country's colonial policy, he found "striking...the extent to which a European education transforms once inoffensive Hindus into ferocious enemies of their masters."[125] Refusing to take Indian nationalism seriously, Le Bon glimpsed a greater danger in the ability of the East, once equipped with machinery through Western investment, to out-produce and under-sell the West. A curious reversal threatened: the old East appeared to be on the verge of a new youth at a time when Europe had begun to encounter old age. Although Indian conditions allowed him to draw back from it at the moment, Le Bon would elaborate that vision in tedious detail in subsequent works. Indeed, he would come to castigate his fellow countrymen for investing in a Trans-Siberian railway which would facilitate the inundation of the French domestic market with cheaply-produced Chinese goods.

Although this vision of an economic yellow peril would come to find adherents, another view of the Chinese and, initially, the Japanese predominated in the nineteenth century. Again Adam Smith had struck the leading note: "China seems to have long been stationary."[126] Biology reinforced political economy when, in discussing the Mongolian race in *Le règne animal, distribué d'aprés son organisation* (1817), Georges Cuvier declared: "Great empires have been established by this race in China and Japan and their conquests have been extended to this side of the Great Desert. In civilization, however, it has always remained stationary."[127] Three years later Shelley proposed that, had it not been for the ancient Greeks, Europe might well have ended up in the same "stagnant and miserable state of social institutions as China and Japan."[128] The English translator of the Chinese classics, James Legge, asserted in 1861: "China's politie has the size of a giant, while it still retains the mind of a child. Its hoary age is but senility."[129] Expressive of a more basic and lasting attitude, this yoking of the infantile and the senile was not altogether unrelated to the second Anglo-Chinese War.

Apparent stagnation invited rapine, often enough for the most benevolent of reasons. On the eve of the second Opium War, the British consul, Rutherford Alcock, after invoking commerce as "the true herald of civilization," declared that "man's efforts at civilization invariably—when the race to be benefited is inferior, intellectually and physically, to the nation civilizing—have but one result, the weaker has gone down before the stronger."[130] During the course of the conflict, Captain Osborn portrayed his government as breaking down "the unrighteous walls of monopoly which bar four hundred million men from European civilization and God's truth."[131] The Chinese response to such benefits eventually exploded in 1900 in the Boxer Rebellion, which prompted an American commentator to proclaim in *Harper's Bazaar* that "the Gatling gun must blaze the way, and shrapnel and shell must knock civilization into the most bigoted and stubborn race in the world."[132] Even the Kaiser, while urging his troops to act as Huns, as savages or barbarians, developed a most un-Germanic dedication to civilization.

It was all too much for Mark Twain who exploded in rage against "the blessings of Civilization Trust."[133] He observed venomously: "Extending the blessings of civilization to our brother who sits in darkness has been a good trade and has paid well, on the whole, and there is money in it yet, if carefully worked."[134] Pointing out that recently Christians had been less than careful, he queried:

> Would it not be prudent to get our civilizing tools
> together and see how much stock is left in hand in the
> way of Glass Beads and Theology, and Maxim Guns and
> Hymn Books, and Trade Gin and Torches of Progress
> and Enlightenment...and balance the books...so that
> we may intelligently decide whether to continue the
> business or sell out the property and start a new Civiliza-
> tion Scheme on the proceeds?[135]

Although he reserved his special animus for the missionaries,
Twain's use of "trust" cut in two directions. As his imagery
recalled, it had a much more directly economic significance in
the world of capitalism. The world of the cartels and the trusts
was very much the world of imperialism. But imperialism, from
early on, possessed an ideological dimension, and the notions
of trust and trusteeship served as justifications for the domination of the uncivilized and semi-civilized.

If Twain mocked James Fenimore Cooper's fiction, he did
share a concern with the man who had thought initially of
calling his *The American Democrat*, "Anti-Cant." Both in their
different fashions excoriated hypocrisy. By the end of the century civilization had become very much an item of cant. The
manner in which the Boxer Rebellion was suppressed only un-
derlined the chasm between reality and the values invoked to
justify that reality. Ideology, emptied of a relation to reality, no
matter how convoluted, inevitably appears as gross hypocrisy.
But it would take World War I to drive that lesson home to
highly civilized Europeans. In the meantime Sigmund Freud,
very much an admirer of Mark Twain, had begun to inves-
tigate the relationship between civilization and hypocrisy, a
relationship which can be best seen in the treatment of those
deemed at or beyond the borders of civilization.

NOTES

1. James Boswell, *Life of Johnson* (London: Oxford University Press, 1969) p. 446.
2. Emile Benveniste, *Problems in General Linguistics*, p. 293. One of Smith's predecessors, Adam Ferguson, issued a warning which, had it been heeded, would have saved much subsequent trouble and confusion: "We are ourselves the supposed standards of politeness and civilization; and where our features do not appear, we apprehend, that there is nothing which deserves to be known." Quoted in Marvin Harris, *The Rise of Anthropological Theory. A History of Theories of Culture* (New York: Thomas Y. Cromwell Co., 1968), p. 29.
3. Another measure of the term's novelty can be found in Gibbon's *The Decline and Fall of the Roman Empire*, the first volume of which also appeared in 1776. The celebrated first sentence of the first chapter has it: "In the second century of the Christian era, the empire of Rome comprehended the fairest part of the earth, and the most civilized portion of mankind." But nowhere in that chapter does he use "civilization" though it occasionally appears later. Edward Gibbon, *The History of the Decline and Fall of the Roman Empire*, I (New York: Heritage Press, n.d.), p. 1.
4. Like other Enlightenment arguments, Millar's cut in two directions. Using the treatment of women as a standard was sensible and humane. But often enough the argument was invoked in the nineteenth century by those who, conveniently forgetting the conditions of factory life and urban prostitution, measured the treatment of their wives and daughters against the "drudgery" of "savage" women and the "perversions" of harem life in the "stationary" civilizations. Sometimes the argument concerned more narrowly conceived professional interests. Thus, writing in the *Lancet* in 1847, Dr. Tyler Smith had it: "The excellence of obstetric medicine is one of the most emphatic expressions of that high regard and estimation in which women are always held by civilized races. The state of the obstetric arts in any country may be taken as a measure of the respect and value of its people for the female sex; and this, in turn, may be taken as a tolerably true indication of the standard of civilization." His stake in the matter emerged in his "hope...that the very term *midwifery* will be rejected." Quoted in Catherine Gallagher and Thomas Laqueur, *The Making of the Human Body: Sexuality and Society in the Nineteenth Century* (Berkeley: University of California Press, 1986), pp. 151, 15.

    The notion of the treatment of women as a measure of civilization would be taken over by non-Westerners who would adopt the general idea for their own uses. Thus, in 1900, the Arab theorist, Qasim Amin, made it integral to his discussion of civilization. Central to that discussion, however, was the fundamental importance of science within genuine civilization.

The appropriation of Western notions of civilization by colonials and non-Westerners lies beyond the confines of this study. Any such discussion would have to take into consideration the differing reasons for appropriation and the uses to which the idea was put. Infected with Anglo-Saxon racism, Canadians would bring British notions of civilization to their treatment of aborigines and others. With the case of the nineteenth-century Argentine politician D.F. Sarmiento being especially revealing in this regard, Latin American Creoles, more influenced by the French, also invoked civilization in their dealing with aborigines and others. Equally important, native agents of imperialism could and did take over, at least in part, the attitudes of those they served. At a time of mass slaughter in Europe, Nigerian clerks apparently believed the March 6, 1915 message of the *Lagos Weekly Record*: "It is idle and fruitless to resist the onward march and insidious influences of Civilization and Progress." I owe that quotation to my Africanist colleague, Michael Mason.

5. Only a few suggestions can be made here regarding the various rejections of civilization. At the most banal level, the primitivist response—on the part, say, of the Melville of *Typee* or Gauguin—was highly dependent upon what they denounced. So too was that on the part of those, ranging from missionaries to rum merchants and gun-runners, who managed to find more permanent satisfactions outside of or on the edge of civilization.

Criticism of civilization from within was of more importance. Such criticism on the part of reformers like John Stuart Mill had to do with the inadequacies of the current condition and implied a perfecting of civilization. Non-primitivist rejection was quite another matter. As early as 1805, an obscure English physician, Charles Hall, advised: "A people who, from extreme civilization, should descend to a medium state, i.e. to one equally distant from their own and that of a savage, would probably be placed in that situation which would be the happiest that human nature is capable of enjoying." For the French arch-conservative, Fréderic Le Play, civilization was "a word introduced in modern times. It is vague and useless, if it simply expresses the state of a people which swarms together...and builds cities. It is false and dangerous, if it implies the idea that massing together implies the model of the Good and the example of Happiness."

The greatest critic of civilization in the nineteenth century was, however, the utopian Charles Fourier. He charged: "the philosophers tell us that civilization is the culmination of social destinies; in fact it is merely the fifth of thirty-two societies, and one of the most wretched." In 1849, Henry James Sr., at once a Swedenborgian and a Fourierist, announced to Boston's staid Town and Country Club: "Between the fundamental idea of Socialism, which offers the possibility of perfect life on earth, and the fundamental idea of Civilization, which affirms the perpetual imperfection of human life, or the permanent subjection of man to nature and society, a great discrepancy exists." Despite ample quotations from Marx and Engels, Edward Carpenter repeated an essentially Fourierist message in his popular *Civilization: Its Cause and Cure* (1889).

Carpenter was a friend of William Morris who, considering himself a Marxist, declared that his "*special* leading motive as a Socialist is hatred to civilization; my ideal of the new Society would not be satisfied unless that Society destroyed civilization." Linking civilization to imperialism, Morris may have been unaware of the sentiments voiced in 1848 by another friend, Frederick Engels: "though the manner in which the brutal soldiers have carried on the war is highly blamable, the conquest of Algeria is an important and fortunate fact for the progress of civilization." Shared by Marx, this perspective lay closer to that of Engel's fellow Manchester merchants than to that of Morris. But Morris came to know Engels at a time when he had begun to reevaluate civilization. In *The Origin of the Family, Private Property and the State* (1884), Engels announced: "I had intended at the outset to place the brilliant critique of civilization, scattered through the works of Fourier by the side of Morgan's and my own." Unfortunately, he neglected Fourier in order to devote attention to the American anthropologist, Lewis Henry Morgan, whose *Ancient Society, or Researches in the Lines of Human Progress from Savagery through Barbarism to Civilization* had appeared in 1877. If Morgan had scant doubts about progress, he also believed that the current state of civilization, resting on property and greed, should and would be transcended. Transcendence was of special importance, for neither Marx nor Engels ever flirted with primitivism.

The critique of civilization, in brief, was every bit as complicated as the idea itself.

Charles Hall, *The Effects of Civilization on the People in European States* (London: T. Ostell and Ch. Chappel, 1805), p. 259; F. Le Play, *La Méthode sociale* (Tours: Alfred Mame et fils, 1879). p. 488; Jonathan Breecher and Richard Bienvenu (eds.), *The Utopian Vision of Charles Fourier: Selected Texts on Work, Love and Passionate Attraction* (Boston: Beacon Press, 1971), p. 103; Henry James, Sr., "Socialism and Civilization," F. O. Matthiessen, *The James Family* (New York: Vintage Books, 1980), pp. 40-58, p. 50; E. P. Thompson, *William Morris, From Romantic to Revolutionary* (London: Merlin Press, 1977), p.718; Frederick Engels, "French Rule in Algeria," Scholmo Avineri (ed.), *Karl Marx on Colonialism and Modernization* (Garden City: Anchor Books, 1969), pp. 47-48, p. 47; and Frederick Engels, *The Origin of the Family, Private Property, and the State* (New York: Pathfinder Press, 1972), fn 1, p. 165.

6. J. R. Seeley, *The Expansion of England* (Chicago: University of Chicago Press, 1971), p. 9.
7. "The Crisis of the Mind," Paul Valéry, *History and Politics, Collected Works*, X (New York: Bollingen Books, 1962), p. 23.
8. Quoted in George A. Panichas (ed.), *Promise of Greatness, The War of 1914-1918* (New York: The John Day Co., 1968), p. 521.
9. "Civilization," Clive Bell, *Civilization and Old Friends* (Chicago: University of Chicago Press, 1955), pp. 5-189, p. 62. Bell dedicated his book to Virginia Woolf who, a decade later, would display a much firmer grasp of the dynamics of civilization in *Three Guineas*.
10. Sigmund Freud, *The Future of an Illusion* (Garden City: Doubleday & Co., 1964), p. 2.
11. Thomas Mann, *Reflections of an Unpolitical man* (New York: Fredrich Ungar, 1983), p.17.
12. Oswald Spengler, *The Decline of the West* (New York: The Modern Library, 1962), p. 182.
13. Quoted in Jan Romein, *The Watershed of Two Worlds: Europe in 1900* (Middletown: Wesleyan University Press, 1978), p.370.
14. Marie J.A.M. de Condorcet, *Sketch for a Historical Picture of the Progress of the Human Mind* (London: Weidenfeld and Nicolson, 1955), pp. 126-127.
15. *Ibid.*, p. 193.
16. "Plan of the Scientific Operations Necessary for Reorganizing Society," Gertrude Lenzer (ed.), *Auguste Comte and Positivism* (New York: Harper & Row, 1975), p.39.
17. *Ibid.*, p. 37.
18. "Cours de Philosophie Positive," excerpted in *Ibid.*, pp. 71-306, p. 280.
19. "The History of Civilization in Europe," excerpted in Stanley Mellon (ed.), *Guizot: Historical Essays and Lectures*, (Chicago: University of Chicago Press, 1972), p.143.
20. *Ibid.*, p. 144.
21. *Ibid.*, p. 165.
22. Quoted in Theodore Zeldin, *France, 1848-1945*, II (Oxford: Oxford University Press, 1977), p. 9.
23. Quoted in *Ibid.*
24. Alexis de Tocqueville, "Journeys to England and Ireland," excerpted in Christopher Hervie, Graham Martin, and Aaron Scharf (eds.), *Industrialization & Culture, 1830-1914* (Glasgow: Macmillan and Co., 1970), pp. 40-24, p. 42.
25. Jules Michelet, *The People* (Urbana: University of Illinois Press, 1973), p. 18.
26. "L'Avenir de la Science," Ernst Renan, *Oeuvres complètes*, III (Paris: Calmann-Lévy, n.d.), p. 1012.
27. Arthur de Gobineau, *Essai sur l'inégalité des races humaines* (Paris: Editions Pierre Belfond, 1967), pp. 109-21.

Civilization

28. *Ibid.*, p. 872. Allied to his racism was a division of nations in terms of whether the intellectual, the female, element or the material, male, element predominated. If Gobineau differed from his contemporaries in assigning primacy of intellectual rather than of moral qualities to women, this kind of thinking was not that unusual. Gustav Klemm, in his massive *Allgemeine Kulturgeschichte der Menscheit* (1843-1852) divided humanity into "active" or male races and "passive" or female races and might have influenced, directly or indirectly, Feuerbach and Bismarck, both of whom coquetted with the idea. The sinister twist which could be given to this kind of argument had already appeared in Gustave d'Eichthal and Ismayl Urbain's *Lettres sur la race noire et la race blanche* (1839), a Saint-Simonian tract which worked out in some detail an equation of blacks with women and whites with males.

29. Th. Funck-Brentano, *La Civilisation et ses lois morales sociales* (Paris: E. Plon et Cie., 1876), pp. 50-51.
30. Quoted in Roger Soltau, *French Political Thought in the Nineteenth Century* (New York: Russell & Russell, 1959), p. 312.
31. Quoted in Raymond Rudorff, *The Belle Epoque: Paris in the Nineties* (New York: Saturday Review Press, 1973), p. 214.
32. Quoted in *Ibid.*, p. 322. From their inception, International Expositions have always provided occasions for the celebration of civilization. Even the Central Europeans had to make concessions on this score.
33. Quoted in Michèle Duchet, *Anthropologie et Histoire au siècle des lumières* (Paris: François Mapero, 1971), p. 218.
34. Quoted in William B. Cohen, *The French Encounter with Africans: White Responses to Blacks, 1530-1880* (Bloomington: University of Indiana Press, 1980), pp. 273-274.
35. Quoted in Raoul Girardet, *L'ideé coloniale en France de 1871 à 1962* (Paris: La Table Ronde, 1972), p. 87.
36. Quoted in Henri Brunschwig, *French Colonialism, 1871-1914: Myths, and Realities* (New York: Frederick J. Praeger, 1964), p. 75.
37. Quoted in *Ibid.*
38. Leopold de Saussure, "Psychologie de colonisation française dans ses rapports avec les societés indigènes," excerpted in Philip D. Curtin (ed.), *Imperialism* (New York: Harper & Row, 1971), pp. 85-92, p. 89. I have argued elsewhere that the differences between the two schools had to do most fundamentally, that is, materially and not ideologically, with such matters as property and labour relations in the colonies. That is not to say, however, that ideology did not play an important role in these quarrels.
39. Quoted in Modris Ekstein, *The Rites of Spring: The Great War and the Birth of the Modern Age* (Toronto: Lester and Orpen Dennys, 1989), pp. 215-16.
40. Thomas Malthus, *An Essay on Population* (New York: W. W. Norton & Co., 1976), pp. 138-39.

41. James Mill, *The History of British India* (Chicago: University of Chicago Press, 1975), p. 224.
42. Quoted in Ruth Richardson, *Death, Dissection and the Destitute* (Harmondsworth: Penguin Books, 1988), p. 156.
43. Quoted in Steven Marcus, *Engels, Manchester, and the Working Class* (New York: Random House, 1974), p. 54.
44. Quoted in Rhoads Murphey, *The Outsiders: The Western Experience in India and China* (Ann Arbor: University of Michigan Press, 1977), p. 22.
45. Quoted in J. B. Bury *The Idea of Progress: An Inquiry into Its Origin and Growth* (New York: Dover Publications, 1955), p. 330.
46. Samuel Taylor Coleridge, *On the Constitution of Church and State, Collected Works* X (Princeton: Princeton University Press, 1976), fn. 2, pp. 42-43.
47. *Ibid.*, pp. 42-43.
48. *Ibid.*, p. 81.
49. *Ibid.*, pp. 48-49.
50. "Civilization," John Stuart Mill, *Essays on Politics and Culture* (Garden City: Doubleday & Co., 1962), p. 51.
51. *Ibid.*,
52. *Ibid.*, p.59.
53. "Modern French Historical Works," John Stuart Mill, *Essays on French History and Historians, Collected Works*, XX (Toronto, University of Toronto Press, 1985), pp. 46, 45.
54. John Stuart Mill, *A System of Logic, Ratiocinative and Inductive. Being a Connected View of the Principles of Evidence and the Methods of Scientific Method*, Books IV-VI, *Collected Works*, VIII (Toronto: University of Toronto Press, 1974), p. 640.
55. John Stuart Mill, *Principles of Political Economy with Some of Their Applications to Social Philosophy*, Books III-IV, *Collected Works*, III (Toronto: University of Toronto Press, 1965), pp. 367-68.
56. John Henry Newman, *The Idea of a University* (Garden City: Image Books, 1959), p. 249.
57. *Ibid.*, p. 251.
58. Matthew Arnold, *Culture & Anarchy* (Cambridge: The University Press, 1960), p. 49.
59. *Ibid.*, p. 47.
60. "Equality," Lionel Trilling (ed.), *The Portable Matthew Arnold* (New York: The Viking Press, 1949), pp. 573-608, p. 584.
61. *Ibid.*
62. *Ibid.*
63. "Friendship's Garland (I)," *The Complete Works of Matthew Arnold*, V (Ann Arbor: University of Michigan Press, 1965), pp. 21-22.
64. Henry Thomas Buckle, *History of Civilization in England*, I (London: Longmans, Green & Co., 1908), p. 152.
65. *Ibid.*, pp. 242-43.

Civilization

66. Edward Burnett Tylor, *The Origin of Culture*, (New York: Harper Torchbooks, 1958), p. 1.
67. *Ibid.*, p. 27.
68. *Ibid.*, p. 31.
69. "The Descent of Man and Selection in Relation to Sex," Charles Darwin, *The Origin of Species and the Descent of Man* (New York: The Modern Library, n.d.), p. 503.
70. Quoted in *Ibid.*, pp. 811-12.
71. *Ibid.*, p. 873.
72. *Ibid.*
73. Quoted in Fawn Brodie, *The Devil Drives: A Life of Sir Richard Burton* (New York: Ballentine Books, 1969), p. 75.
74. "Physics and Politics," Walter Bagehot, *Collected Works*, VII (London: The Economist, 1974), pp. 17-144, p. 106.
75. Benjamin Kidd, *The Control of the Tropics* (New York: The Macmillan Co., 1898), p.53.
76. Quoted in Samuel Hynes, *The Edwardian Turn of Mind* (Princeton: Princeton University Press, 1968), p.32.
77. C.F.G. Masterman, *The Condition of England* (London: Methuen & Co., 1960), pp. 166-67.
78. Bell, "Civilization," p. 13.
79. Quoted in Roy Harvey Pearce, *The Savages of America: A Study of the Indian and the Idea of Civilization* (Baltimore: The Johns Hopkins Press, 1981), p. 89.
80. Quoted in Reginald Horseman, *Race and Manifest Destiny: The Origins of American Racial Anglo-Saxonism* (Cambridge: Harvard University Press, 1981), p. 89.
81. Quoted in Frederick Merk, *Manifest Destiny and Mission in American History* (New York: Alfred A. Knopf, 1963). p. 126.
82. Quoted in Edward McNall Burns, *The American Idea of Mission: Concepts of National Purpose and Destiny* (New Brunswick: Rutgers University Press, 1957), p. 7.
83. Quoted in *Ibid.*, p. 218.
84. Quoted in Robert Drinnon, *Facing West: The Metaphysics of Indian-Hating and Empire Building* (Minneapolis: University of Minnesota Press, 1980), p. 349. The advertisement goes some way to justify Heinrich von Treitschke's jibe: "The English think Soap is civilization." Quoted in G.M. Young, *Victorian England: Portrait of an Age* (New York: Oxford University Press, 1964), p. 24. Freud took seriously the relationship between cleanliness and civilization.
85. Josiah Strong, *Our Country: Its Possible Future and the Present Crisis* (Cambridge: Belnap Press, 1963), p. 205.
86. *Ibid.*
87. "Civilization," Ralph Waldo Emerson, *Society and Solitude* (Boston: Houghton, Mifflin and Co., 1904), pp. 17.

88. *Ibid.*, p. 19.
89. *Ibid.*, p. 21.
90. *Ibid.*, p. 31.
91. Henry Adams, *The Education of Henry Adams* (New York: Modern Library, 1931), p.91.
92. Quoted in T.J. Jackson Lears, *No Place of Grace: Antimodernism and the Transformation of American Culture, 1880-1920* (New York: Pantheon Books, 1981), p. 54.
93. Alexis de Tocqueville, *Democracy in America*, I (New York: Vintage Books, 1954), p. 439.
94. *Ibid.*, pp. 123, 36.
95. Quoted in Antonelli Gerbi, *The Dispute of the New World: The History of a Polemic, 1750-1900* (Pittsburgh: University of Pittsburgh Press, 1973), p. 463.
96. Louis Galantière (ed.), *The Goncourt Journals* (Garden City: Doubleday Anchor, 1958), p. 233
97. "Civilization in the United States," *The Complete Works of Matthew Arnold*, IX, (Ann Arbor: University of Michigan Press, 1977), pp. 352-53.
98. *Ibid.*, p. 355.
99. *Ibid.*, p. 363.
100. Quoted in Noel Annan, *Leslie Stephen: The Godless Victorian* (New York: Random House, 1984), p. 289.
101. Quoted in Howard Becker and Harry Elmer Barnes, *Social Thought from Lore to Science: A History and Interpretation of Man's Ideas about Life with His Fellows*, II, (Washington: Harren Press, 1952), p. 1036.
102. Quoted in Isaiah Berlin, *Russian Thinkers* ((Harmondsworth: Penguin Books, 1979), p. 98.
103. Quoted in Hans Kohn, *Pan-Slavism: Its History and Ideology* (New York: Vintage Books, 1960), p. 139.
104. Quoted in *Ibid.*, p. 29.
105. Quoted in Duchet, *Anthropologie et Histoire*, p. 224.
106. Marquis de Custine, *Empire of the Czar: A Journey Through Eternal Russia* (New York: Anchor Books, 1989), pp. 71, 128.
107. *Ibid.*, p. 278.
108. Quoted in Kohn, *Pan-Slavism*, p. 113.
109. Henry Rawlinson, *England and Russia and the East. A Series of Papers on the Political and Geographical Condition of Central Asia* (New York: Praeger Publishers, 1970), p. 142.
110. Quoted in Lytton Strachey, *Queen Victoria* (New York: Harcourt, Brace & World, 1921), p. 363.
111. "History of Civilization in France," excerpted in Mellon (ed.). *Guizot*, pp. 268-69.
112. Buckle, *History of Civilization in England*, II, p. 126.

113. Quoted in John Field, *Toward A Programme of Imperial Life: The British Empire at the Turn of the Century* (Westport: Greenwood Press, 1982), p. 163.
114. The Earl of Cromer, *Modern Egypt*, II (New York: Macmillan, 1908), p. 238.
115. *Ibid.*, p. 538.
116. *Ibid.*, p. 539.
117. Gobineau to Tocqueville, Jan. 15, 1856, Alexis de Tocqueville, *"The European Revolution" & Correspondence with Gobineau* (Garden City: Anchor Books, 1959), pp. 278-79.
118. Quoted in Raymond Dawson, *The Chinese Chameleon: An Analysis of European Conceptions of Chinese Civilization* (London: Oxford University Press, 1967), p. 66
119. James Mill, *History of British India*, p. 228.
120. *Ibid.* Although more devoted to liberty than utility, John Stuart Mill explained: "The Egyptian hierarchy, the paternal despotism of China, were very fit instruments for carrying those nations up to the point of civilization which they attained. But having reached that point, they were brought to a permanent halt for want of mental liberty and individuality; requisites of improvement which the institutions that had carried them thus far entirely incapacitated them from acquiring; and as the institutions did not break down and give place to others, further improvement stopped." Mill, "Representative Government," p. 268.
121. Karl Marx, "The British Rule in India," Avineri (ed.), *Karl Marx*, p. 111.
122. Bagehot, "Physics and Politics," pp. 106, 99.
123. *Ibid.*, p. 107.
124. Gustave Le Bon, *Les Civilisations de l'Inde* (Paris: Librairie Firmin-Dido et Cie., 1887), p. 718.
125. *Ibid.*, p. 711.
126. Adam Smith, *An Inquiry into the Nature and Causes of the Wealth of Nations*, I (Indianapolis: Liberty Classics, 1981), p. 111.
127. Excerpted in Curtin (ed), *Imperialism*, pp. 4-12, p. 8.
128. Quoted in V. G. Kiernan, *The Lords of Human Kind: European attitudes to the outside world in the imperial age* (Harmondsworth: Penguin Books, 1972), p. 155.
129. Quoted in Dawson, *Chinese Chameleon*, p. 68.
130. Quoted in Murphey, *Outsiders*, p. 33.
131. Quoted in Kiernan, *Lords*, p. 159.
132. Quoted in Robert McClellan, *The Heathen Chinese: A Study of American Attitudes toward China, 1890-1905* (Columbus: Ohio State University Press, 1971), p. 233.
133. "To the Person Sitting in Darkness," Bernard de Voto (ed.), *The Portable Mark Twain* (New York: Penguin Books, 1977), p. 599.
134. *Ibid.*
135. *Ibid.*, pp. 598-99.

2

CIVILIZATION AND ITS DISCONTENTED

THE NOTION OF CIVILIZATION long predated the word itself, which only entered Western vocabularies in the second half of the eighteenth century. The yoking together of the new noun and a much older sense of cultural superiority at roughly the same time in France and England marked not only a new consciousness of the refinement of manners with which civilization was associated initially, but also a sharpening of the sense of distinction which allowed the self-proclaimed civilized to distance themselves from those designated as uncivilized or semi-civilized: the "savages" abroad or on the frontier; the "savages" at home, the labouring classes, criminals, the insane, women; and the mobs or crowds which managed to subsume most or all of the features of the other groups. While interpretations of civilization ranged from the militantly Christian to the aggressively materialist, its proponents, usually bourgeois males, agreed that it rested upon control: control of self, of Nature, of those whose real or potential discontents fixed them beyond or at the margins of civilization.

Covering a variety of interests, civilization functioned as a hegemonic value which served as a standard of judgment during the nineteenth century when, despite increasing professionalization, specialists were still likely to be conversant with fields of knowledge other than their own. Defined with various degrees of precision, the much lauded notion of civilization was plunged into crisis by World War I, a crisis from which it was only rescued by Freud's reformulation of it in *Civilization and Its Discontents* (1930), a work more congruent with the especially grim conditions of the twentieth century.

Each group cast beyond the pale or located at the margins of civilization was defined by characteristics specific unto itself. Leaving aside the nuances developed by specialists, the common wisdom had it that savages were characterized by stupidity and ferocity; the labouring classes by promiscuity and lack of foresight; criminals, by a lack of respect for the majesty of the law; the insane, by the abandonment of reason; women, by exceptional emotionalism; and the crowd, by a combination of these elements. Not only did such characteristics often overlap, but they all stood basically for the obverse of civilization in that they indicated lack of self-control which, in turn, signalled a dangerous proximity to Nature, essentially that animal nature of humans which civilization sought to curb, to refine, and, very revealingly, to domesticate. Hence, these different groups could be readily equated with each other. While the more specific features which defined each group's distance from civilization, especially when measured in terms of its vulnerability to extermination, will be considered in this essay, the primary focus will be on the process of equation.

Savages, the aboriginal peoples of the world, represented the complete antithesis of the civilized which partially explains why, though other groups were often compared to them, they were seldom compared to groups other than children and wild animals. The comparison with children implied a low level of mental and moral powers, but also held out the possibility of future development. The second comparison, however, could end in calls for extirpation. The discussion of savages, in any event, took place at several levels of discourse.

Savages were referred to in passing by those primarily concerned with other matters: Edward Gibbon and Adam Smith, for instance, made scant use of the neologism "civilization," but had to take into account barbarism and savagery. The metahistorical schema which proliferated in the nineteenth century demanded more urgently integrations of the savage state. According to Auguste Comte, savages suffered no more than children from the boredom which stimulated mental activity. Unwilling to work, these larger children found escape from boredom in warfare. Immensely concerned with the transition from military to industrial activity, Herbert Spencer went out of his way in *The Study of Sociology* (1873) to refute charges of savage cruelty and to recount instances of the atrocities inflicted upon the uncivilized by the civilized. But his basic view had already been expressed in *The Principles of Psychology* (1855) where smaller brain size and simplicity of the nervous system were used to explain the operations of the savage intellect, "sudden in its inferences, incapable of balancing evidence, and adhering obstinately to first impression."[1] Significantly, Spencer also cited such factors when discussing class and gender differences within his own society. By the end of the century, these kinds of observations would be buttressed by a vastly expanded travel literature and the more systematic works of the anthropologists.

Dissatisfaction with travel literature accounted in part for the emergence of anthropology. Aiming at greater precision, the Ideologue, Joseph-Marie de Gérondo, indicated in 1800

49

some of the matters with which ethnographers should be concerned: "the status of women...modesty...love...and the moral education of infants."[2] But already the discovery in 1799 of Victor, the savage or wild-boy of Aveyron, had seemed to provide a better opportunity to test Ideologue assumptions. Refusing to follow his fellow-Ideologue, the psychiatrist, Philippe Pinel, in writing Victor off as an idiot, the physician, Jean-Marc-Gaspard Itard, believed his feral charge to be as close to a *tabula rasa* as one could find. Having taken over Victor's tutoring, Itard was keenly aware of what was at stake:

> Cast upon the globe without physical strength or innate ideas, incapable in himself of obeying the fundamental laws of his nature which call him to the supreme place in the universe, it is only in the heart of society that man can attain the preeminent position which is his natural destiny. Without the aid of civilization he would be one of the feeblest and least intelligent of animals—a statement which has been many times repeated...but which has never been strictly proven.[33]

He concluded, perhaps predictably, from his work with Victor that "the moral responsibility said to be *natural* to man is only the result of civilization."[4] Priding himself on having destroyed Rousseau's charges against civilization, a word which Rousseau had not possessed, Itard still had to recognize the role which the fear of corporal punishment had played in civilizing Victor: it had taught him to steal cunningly. Itard overlooked this all too Rousseauian point in concluding that in this case "the changes wrought by civilization...have brought to light some of the feelings which constitute what has been called righteousness."[5]

While the Ideologues had managed to balance physiological and environmental concerns, the former, frequently interpreted along racist lines, soon came to predominate in France. Systematized in 1817 by the biologist, Georges Cuvier, this tendency was carried further by W. F. Edwards whose *Des caractères physiologiques des races humaines consideré des dans leurs rapports avec l'histoire* appeared in 1829. It influenced, among others, the Saint-Simonians, one of whom developed a racist aesthetics: "the more beautiful a race is, the more its civilization is advanced; the uglier a race is, the more imperfect its civilization."[6] The way lay open for the reign of Paul Broca and his school of physical anthropology. At once a fine scientist and a polygeneticist obsessed with cranial measurement, Broca argued: "A group with a black skin, woolly hair and a prognathous face has never been able to raise itself to civilization."[7]

By 1858, when the Société de anthropologie was founded and *The Origin of Species* published, two things had become clear about the French which had implications for their depictions of savages. First, despite a common emphasis upon the grandeur of their own civilization, a chasm divided the spokesmen for the dominant culture and for most of the anthropologists. The former were assimilative and, at least by implication, evolutionary in their orientation, the latter racist, even to the extent of positing polygenesis. Second, these different perspectives still allowed for a common hostility to Darwinian ideas. The proponents of the assimilative orientation, essentially bourgeois republicans, disliked Darwin's emphasis on brutal struggle. The physical anthropologists, on the other hand, disliked his stressing monogenesis. The latter distaste had appeared as early as 1829 when Edwards had attacked the work of James Cowles Prichard.

A psychiatrist and anthropologist, Prichard lost control over his material as his *Researches into the Physical History of Man* grew from the single volume of 1813, to the two volumes of 1826, to the five volumes of 1848. While his emphasis upon the physical might have had its appeal to French theorists, Prichard's championing of monogenesis created problems for them. Flirting in his own fashion with racism, the Englishman posited that, while the earliest humans had been black, "Wherever we see any progress toward civilization, there we also find deviation towards lighter colour."[8] As for "Cultivation or Civilization," he maintained that "civilized life holds the same relation to the conditions of savages in the human race, which the domesticated state holds to the natural or wild condition among the inferior animals."[9]

A concern with the moral dimension of savage life characterized British anthropology throughout the Victorian years. It reflected in part the extent to which British ethnographers related their endeavours to their own society. Rejecting Rousseauian notions of the noble savage, Sir John Lubbock ended his *Origins of Civilization* (1870) with the hope of extending "the blessings of civilization" not only to the savages abroad, but to "countrymen of our own living, in our midst, a life worse than that of a savage."[10] Sharing such sentiments, J.F. McLennan found in London "predatory bands, leading the life of the lowest nomads" and every phase in the development of family life "from the lowest incestuous combinations of kindred to the highest group based on solemn monogamous marriage."[11] Savagery was none too distant in either time or space: "Savages are unrestrained by any sense of delicacy from copartnery in sexual enjoyments; and, indeed, in the civilized state, the sin of great cities shows no natural restraint sufficient to hold man back from the grosser copartneries."[12] But according to Edward B. Tylor, such views unduly maligned savages:

> If we have to strike a balance between the Papuans...
> and the communities of European beggars and
> thieves, we may readily acknowledge that we have in

our midst something worse than savagery. But it is not savagery, it is broken-down civilization....To my mind the popular phrases about 'city-savages' and 'street arabs' seem like comparing a ruined house to a builder's yard.[13]

In other words, genuine savages, if they managed to survive, were capable of further evolution. But fully willing to "apply the often-repeated comparison of savages to children in their moral and intellectual condition," he found the savage state of mind to be "intermediate between the condition of a healthy prosaic modern citizen and of a raving fanatic or a patient in a fever ward."[14]

Darwin, especially in *The Descent of Man* (1871), drew freely on the work of the anthropologists. Thoroughly conventional outside the realm of biology, he used their work to reinforce opinions in regard to savagery and civilization which had been expressed as early as *The Voyage of the Beagle* (1839). Although he recognized the common humanity of the Fuegians encountered aboard ship, he reacted with shock to the inhabitants of Tierra del Fuego: "I could not have believed the difference between savage and civilized man; it is greater than between a wild and a domesticated animal."[15] Bourgeois truisms explained the difference: the Fuegians suffered from egalitarianism and a lack of private property. Although still far from formulating the theory of natural selection, he reflected more generally: "Whenever the European has trod, death seems to pursue the aboriginal....The varieties of men seem to act on each other in the same way as different species of animals—the stronger always extirpating the weaker."[16]

If he had excellent reasons for largely ignoring humans in his most famous work, Darwin returned to his earlier concerns in *The Descent of Man* where he attempted to balance the general interests of the human species against the particular interests of its components. His evolutionary theory provided grounds for cheer of a sort: if Europeans had managed to reach civilization, then presumably others, if granted sufficient time, could also do so. The problem was that they might not have enough time at their disposal. While allowing for the protection provided some "barbarians" by "a deadly climate," Darwin maintained that "at some future period, not very distant when measured by centuries, the civilized races of man will almost certainly eliminate, and replace, the savage races throughout the world."[17] Invoking Broca's studies of brain size, he also pointed to biological differences in accounting for intellectual and moral differences, the latter of special interest to this good Victorian.

Yet, the very morality which distinguished civilization also threatened it. With the development of civilization, the power of natural selection receded before the advance of sexual selection, and the latter did not necessarily work to the good of the species. Darwin quoted W. R. Greg with approval: "The careless, squalid, unaspiring Irishman multiplies like rabbits; the frugal, foreseeing, self-respecting Scot...passes his best years in struggle and celibacy, marries late, and leaves few behind him."[18] Self-command and self-respect, those marks of civilization, entailed costs. Trying to frame the larger picture, Darwin argued: "With savages, the weak in body were soon eliminated....We civilized men, on the other hand, do our utmost to check the process of elimination; we build asylums for the imbeciles, the maimed and the sick; we institute poor laws and our medical men exert their utmost skill to save the life of everybody to the last moment."[19] Believing it to be impossible to check humanitarian sentiment in civilized conditions, he took what comfort he could in the notion that:

> ...some elimination of the worst dispositions is always
> in progress even in the most civilized nations. Male-

factors are executed, or imprisoned for long periods, so that they cannot freely transmit their bad qualities. Melancholic and insane persons are confined, or commit suicide. Violent and quarrelsome men often come to a bloody end. The restless who will not follow an occupation—and this relic of barbarism is a great check to civilization—emigrate to newly-settled countries, where they prove useful pioneers. Intemperance is highly destructive.... Profligate women bear few children, and profligate men rarely marry; both suffer from disease.[20]

Despite such value-charged judgments, or perhaps because of them, Darwin managed to preserve the aura of the disinterested scientist.

The co-discoverer of evolution, Alfred R. Wallace, found it more difficult to do so. True, he could end coldly his account of the disappearance of the Tasmanian aborigines and speculate dispassionately on the chances of survival of other such groups. But he was a progressive, an improver, a civilizer. He enthused over the prospects for agricultural development held out in Brazil. Convinced, like so many of his contemporaries, of the drudgery inflicted among savage women by savage males, he argued in the usual fashion that "one of the surest and most beneficial effect of advancing civilization, will be the amelioration of the condition of these women."[21] He urged missionaries working the Celebes to persuade "married women to confine themselves to domestic duties" as a way of promoting "a higher civilization."[22] Yet doubts remained. He pondered, in bad verse, the relative merits of savagery and civilization.[23] More forcefully, he urged: "Compared with our wondrous progress in physical science and its practical applications, our system of government, of administering justice, of national education, and our whole social and moral organization, remains in a state of barbarism."[24] Arguing that "our best thinkers" had projected a social state in which "every man would have a sufficiently well-balanced intellectual organization to understand the moral law...and would require no other motive but the free impulses of his own nature to obey that law." Wallace reflected that "among people in a very low state of civilization we find some approach to such a perfect social state."[25]

The American anthropologist, Lewis Henry Morgan, shared Wallace's heretical inclinations. He celebrated in *Ancient Society* (1877) the

> ...common principle of intelligence...in the savage, in the barbarian, and in the civilized man....There is something grandly impressive in a principle which has wrought our civilization from small beginnings; from the arrow head, which expresses the thought in the brain of a savage, to the smelting of iron, which represents the higher intelligence of barbarism, and, finally, to the railway train...which may be called the triumph of civilization.[26]

Respecting railways enough to invest in them, he credited the "greed of gain" with creating the conditions of civilization.[27] But believing that property had become "an unmanageable power," he looked forward to a time "when human intelligence will rise to mastery over property, and define the relations of the state to the property it protects, as well as the obligations and the limits of the rights of its owners."[28]

Such views were not widely shared. According to *The Saturday Review* in 1876, savage life was "a combination of the seamy side of the gamekeeper's profession and of the gypsy's business, with a considerable dash of the discomfort of a pauper lunatic asylum without keepers."[29] Comparisons continued down the evolutionary scale. According to Darwin's German follower, Ernst Haeckel, "since the 'lower races'...are psychologically nearer to mammals (apes and dogs)than to civilized Europeans, we must...assign a totally different value to their lives."[30] It was but a short step from there to the position of the philosopher, Eduard von Hartmann: "No power on earth is able to arrest the eradication of the inferior races of mankind....The true philanthropist, if he has comprehended the natural law of anthropological evolution, cannot avoid desiring an acceleration of the last convulsions, and labouring for that end."[31] Such sentiments were hardly peculiarly German.[32] While all too common, they were the extreme expression of a spectrum of adverse opinion directed against all aboriginal groups, only two of which, black Africans and Amerindians, can be considered here.

While it was conceded that some African groups might go under in the confrontation with civilization, Africans were usually exempted from the possibility of annihilation. Here Christian sentiments, along with the more hard-headed consideration of the need for labour in order to exploit the resources of Africa, came into play. Debate continued to rage, however, over whether back Africans were capable of becoming civilized and, if so, to what extent.

Christians could be patronizing. The Church Missionary Society in 1906 urged Sunday School teachers: "Contrast the darkness of Africa with the light of civilization in England. Shew how applicable the title 'The Dark Continent' is to Africa, as exhibited by the Negro race, as the 'Great Unknown Land,' and as the Country that, more than any other, has been given over to 'Works of Darkness.'"[33] The comparison of Africans, pagans and converts alike, with children came to the missionaries easily enough. But, in their own fashion, they raised serious questions. They debated, for instance, whether Christianity should pave the way for civilization or civilization, the way for Christianity. They usually preferred the first alternative, an indication that they had doubts about the accomplishments of a civilization divorced from Christianity.

That great missionary, David Livingstone, exemplified the ambiguities of their positions. He could sound much like his fellows when it came to Africans: "They are mere children."[34] Nor did he have any doubt that the difference between black and white resembled that between "the lowest and the highest in England."[35] But comparison did not always work to the benefit of his countrymen:

> Not a single improper or imprudent expression from a black woman ever met my ear during a residence of fifteen years among the Bechunas. I should not have been able to say the same had I been a missionary in London. A white man of good 'common sense' may expect kind and civil treatment throughout the interior till he comes upon the borders of what we call civilization.[36]

While this view raised the always delicate question of the conditions of frontier society, Livingstone more generally avoided claims to be civilizing the Africans.

Mary Kingsley, the West African explorer, had scant use for missionaries. Her irreverence touched not only them, but her countrymen, much ethnographical literature, and, most charmingly, herself. While her *Travels in West Africa* (1897) makes for a pleasant contrast to the pompous and often brutal pronouncements of others, it is not without its contradictions. She had no use for the comparison of the African with a satanic child. And again comparison did not necessarily work to the advantage of her fellow-Britons:

> ...there is not one quarter the amount of drunkenness you can see any Saturday night...in the Vauxhall

Road; and you will not find in a whole year's investigation..one seventieth part of the evil, degradation,
and premature decay you can see...in the more dense-
ly populated parts of our towns.[37]

Sceptical of the ways used to introduce civilization to Africans,
she was herself implicated in what some saw as the most vital
work of civilization through her calls for the extension of trade
and the establishment of plantations. Yet, there was civilization and civilization or, as she phrased the matter,

> I do not believe that the white race will ever drag the
> black up to their own particular summit in the moun-
> tain range of civilization. Both polygamy and slavery
> are...essential to the well-being of Africa, and these two
> institutions will necessitate the African having a sum-
> mit to himself. Only—alas for the energetic reformer—
> the African is not keen on mountaineering in the
> civilization range.[38]

While this had to do with the racial inferiority of all non-
Caucasian groups, Africans had a strength of their own: they
increased in numbers rather than died off like other aboriginal
groups when exposed to civilization.

The stark choice between assimilation and extirpation, between civilization and extermination, was foisted upon the
Amerindians of the United States almost as soon as the
neologism and the new republic appeared. It took little time to
achieve such brutal clarity, for already in 1779 the soldiers sent
to fight against the Iroquois who were fighting for the British,
celebrated July 4, the third anniversary of the Declaration of
Independence, with the toast: "Civilization or death to all
savages."[39] In the following decade the author of the Declaration, Thomas Jefferson, replied to European detractors of the

Amerindians in his *Notes on the State of Virginia*: these savages were strong, brave, intelligent and eloquent. There were but two rubs: like other savages, they mistreated their women, and they seemed all too vulnerable to extinction. One motive for his later purchase of the Louisiana Territory was to preserve them by moving them to the west of the Mississippi.

Before the transfer was carried out other measures were taken. In 1819, the Congress set up the Civilization Fund which provided $10,000 annually for the education of the Amerindians in the ways of white culture. With Amerindian matters at that point under the supervision of the War Department, Secretary John C. Calhoun explained in 1820: "They should be taken under our guardianship, and our opinion, and not theirs, ought to prevail in measures intended for their civilization and happiness. A system less vigorous may protract, but cannot avert their fate."[40] Subsequent reports of the Commissioners of Indian Affairs made clear the extent to which their notion of civilization rested upon Lockean principles: "ownership of property," the ability "to make fences, plough and cultivate the fields."[41] While the fence made an excellent symbol of civilization, Christianity also entered into the matter. But neither the sanctity of property nor Christian principles prevented the dispossession of the Amerindians of the American Southeast. In varying degrees literate and Christian, the Cherokees, Creeks, Choctaws, Chickasaws and Seminoles owned property, including slaves, and cultivated land. Their degree of civilization, however, did not spare them the attention of whites who saw in their lands the potential for cotton cultivation. Their brutal removal to the west of the Mississippi cleared the way for such cultivation and the civilization which it would support.

None of this is to say that the Amerindians did not find white champions. Perhaps the most understanding of these was George Catlin who in 1841 published his *Letters and Notes on the Manners, Customs and Conditions of the North American Indians.* No sentimentalist, he understood such matters as the role of inter-tribal warfare. But finding Amerindians to be "the most honest and honorable race of people I have ever lived amongst," he doubted whether civilization had much to offer them.[42] He concentrated his hatred on the frontier, "the fleeting and unsettled line...which indefinitely separates civilized from Indian population—a moving barrier, where the unrestrained and natural propensities of two people are concentrated, in an atmosphere of lawless inequity."[43] Although prepared to be sympathetic, others proved less understanding. Three years after the appearance of Catlin's book, the feminist and abolitionist, Margaret Fuller, returned to the familiar theme of the treatment of Amerindian women in order to rank Amerindians as inferior to Europeans. Her future employer, Horace Greeley, actually found grounds for hope in the status of these women: "Degraded and filthy as they are...they bear the germ of renovation for their race, in that they are neither too proud nor too indolent to labor."[44] The obsession with that mark of civilization, labour, could be carried in different directions. The great black abolitionist, Frederick Douglass, proclaimed in 1854: "The Indian dies, under the flashing glance of the Anglo-Saxon. Not so the Negro: civilization cannot kill him. He embraces it—becomes a part of it."[45] What part of civilization remained at issue. Casting his interpretation in terms of the black capacity for labour, the pro-slavery, George Fitzhugh, proclaimed: "The Indian...is doomed to extinction."[46]

At one with Fitzhugh in scientistic pretension, the racist Josiah Nott had already asserted that the Amerindian was "an untameable, carnivorous animal which is fading away before civilization."[47] In 1852 a Californian urged the acceleration of the process: "Providence designed the extermination of the Indian and...it would be a good thing to introduce the small pox among them."[48] The outcome of the Civil War did nothing to temper such sentiments. Confronted with complaints about the slaughter of the buffalo so necessary to the existence of the Great Plains aborigines, General Philip Sheridan replied: "Let them kill, skin, and sell until the buffalo is exterminated...it is the only way to bring lasting peace and allow civilization to advance."[49]

Assimilationists could be harsh in their own manner. The founder of the Carlisle Indian School announced in 1883: "In Indian civilization I am a Baptist because I believe in immersing them in our civilization and when we get them under holding them there until they are thoroughly soaked."[50] Perhaps "bleached" would have been a better verb. In any event, in 1887 the Reverend Lyman Abbert produced a formula which covered the perspectives of both exterminators and assimilators and summed up more than a century of Caucasian American experience: "Barbarism has no rights which civilization is bound to respect."[51] Years earlier, reviewing a new edition of the works of James Fenimore Cooper, the historian, Francis Parkman, had come up with an equally pithy formula: "Civilization has a destroying as well as a creating power."[52]

Cooper's relevance for some European novelists went beyond his literary skills. In 1828 Balzac depicted the Bretons of *Les Chouans* as "Mohicans" and "Red Skins." A protagonist of *Paysans* (1844) mused: "You don't need to go to America to see savages. Here are the Redskins of Fenimore Cooper."[53] In *Cousin Bette* (1847-1848) the novelist spelled out a fundamental distinction: "The savage only has sentiments, the civilized man has sentiments and ideas."[54] If Balzac's view encompassed both countryside and city, Eugene Sue's perspective was distinctly urban. In introducing *Les Mystères de Paris* (1843) he warned:

> We are about to place before the reader some episodes in the life of barbarians as far outside civilization as the savage hordes so well depicted by Cooper. Only the barbarians we are speaking of are in our midst....

These men have manners of their own, women of their own, a mysterious language replete with baleful images, metaphors dripping with blood. Like the savages, these people usually address each other by nicknames borrowed from their energy, their cruelty or certain physical qualities or defects.[55]

If the democratic Michelet accused Balzac and Sue of being excessively preoccupied with "the bizarre, the exceptional, the monstrous," the comparisons were more than literary conceits.[56] They were the common coin of social observation and commentary.

Echoing views already expressed in the seventeenth century, a Limousin landowner described peasants as "animals with two feet, hardly resembling a man....The wild dull gaze betrays no flicker of thought in the brain of this being, morally and physically atrophied."[57] Such sentiments invited comparisons between the rural population at home and those of the colonial sphere: both were frequently portrayed as somewhat less than human. The matter was further complicated by the Second Empire's use of rural votes to reinforce Bonapartist power. In the wake of the defeat at Sedan, Renan blamed the "peasants—the very dregs of civilization—who were responsible for inflicting that government on us for twenty years."[57] Committed for different reasons to universal manhood suffrage, the bourgeois masters of the Third Republic faced the challenge of republicanizing and secularizing—that is, civilizing—the peasantry without stripping it of a fundamental social conservatism. The educational programme of the Republic entailed, in brief, an internal *mission civilisatrice*.

That effort was directed as much towards urban workers as towards the peasants. If the latter were often depicted as savages and barbarians, they did not stir the same degree of fear as the urban *classes laborieuses* who by the early nineteenth century had been identified as the *classes dangereuses*. H.-A. Frégier spelled out the message in *Des classes dangereuses de la population dans les grandes villes et des moyens de les rendre meilleures* (1840). But already in 1831 the journalist Saint-Marc Girardin, had proclaimed: "The barbarians who menace society are neither in the Caucasus nor on the steppes of Tartary: they are in the suburbs of our manufacturing towns."[59] The liberal economist, Charles Dunoyer, deplored the "vivacity...drunkenness...incontinence...idleness...excessive lack of foresight of savages" before supplying the vision of "civilization menaced with new barbarians...not this time from the polar regions, but from the inferior ranks of society."[60]

The revolutionary events of 1848 threatened the realization of that vision. At the end of April the staid *Revue des deux mondes* proclaimed: "Socialism is barbarism."[61] A month later *Le Constitutionnel* presented society as divided between the forces of "order, liberty, civilization, the great Revolution of France" and "some madmen emerging to massacre and pillage...new barbarians" who attacked "families, institutions, liberty, country...the civilization of the XIXth century."[62] General Bugeaud, who had gained his reputation extending civilization in Algeria, was more succinct: the revolutionaries of the June Days were "the new Vandals."[63] More than two decades later the Commune deepened such fears. Edmund de Goncourt found what comfort he could in reflecting: "Perhaps in the great law of change that governs all earthly things, the workers are for modern civilization what the barbarians were for ancient society, the convulsive agents of dissolution and destruction."[64] The Commune also terrified Maxime du Camp who depicted its instigators as "aiming right at the heart of civilization."[65] Its success, he believed, would have meant "a return to barbarism," the barbarism of "the stone age."[66]

The antithesis between proletarian savagery and bourgeois civilization would continue to be invoked during the

Third Republic, with a new element appearing in the willing-
ness of some anarchists to identify themselves proudly as barbarians. Curiously, while fears of the revolutionary potential
of the proletariat were real enough, the French seldom moved
from the savagery-civilization dichotomy to a "two nation"
perspective. Nationalism was too strong, especially among
republicans, to tolerate such an internal division. Faith in the
power of education, again especially strong among
republicans, also held out the prospect of the eventual civilization of the internal savages. Moreover, although tendencies in
that direction can be detected, especially among conservatives,
the French never produced critics of urban life comparable to
those who flourished so freely in England and Germany.
French thought on the matter had a logic of its own: France
was the centre of civilization; Paris was the centre of France;
hence, whatever the shortcomings of its inhabitants, Paris was
the true centre of civilization.

Such logic, however, did not prevent the drawing of comparisons with conditions elsewhere. Eugène Buret concluded
in *La misère des classes laborieuses en France et en Angleterre* (1840)
that in both countries "the laboring classes are gradually ex-
pelled from the usage and laws of civilized life and reduced to
the state of barbarism through the sufferings and privations of
destitution."[67] He charged that "in the home of civilization,
you will encounter thousands of men reduced by sheer besot-
tedness to a life of savagery."[68] The African analogy came readily to mind: "Savages alone take to drink with the fervor
displayed by the most degraded part of the poor classes, like
the Negro on the African coast who will sell his children and
himself for a bottle of spirits."[69] He had no difficulty in finding
other parallels. Not only did workers lead nomadic lives like
savages, but the fundamental conditions of their existence
were the same: "The life of the individual proletarian and the
savage alike is at the mercy of the hazards of life, the whims of

chance; one day good hunting or wages, the next day no game or unemployment; plenty one day, famine the next."[70] While sympathetic to the plight of the workers, Buret did not hesitate to categorize paupers as "the enemies of civilization."[71]

Always willing to learn from the experiences of others, Tocqueville had already turned his attention to the paupers of England. Reporting to the Chambre in 1835 on the recent English Poor Law, he warned that, breaking the connections between rich and poor, it produced "two rival nations."[72] This "two nations" thesis found greater support in the English-speaking world than in his own France. In 1841 the Boston Unitarian, William Channing, proposed that "in most large cities there may be said to be two nations, understanding as little of one another, having as little intercourse as if they lived in different lands."[73] Not altogether surprisingly, he had discovered London suburbs which could be compared to African villages. Disraeli's *Sybil* (1844) lent the thesis even greater currency. Although he presented the matter in general terms of rich and poor, it rapidly acquired an urban focus, for in nineteenth century Britain, the problems posed by cities, whether new industrial cities like Manchester or the world metropolis of London, simply could not be ignored. Much of what was said and written about them was highly critical, though a distinction must be made between those who condemned wholly and those who aimed at the amelioration of urban conditions. In either case, just as with the celebrants of urban life, the question of civilization entered into the matter: for Robert Southey, cities destroyed civilization; for Robert Vaughan, they fostered it.

Manchester provided the test case of the new industrial city. *Chamber's Edinburgh Journal* celebrated it in 1858: "Manchester's streets may be irregular, and its trading inscriptions pretentious, its smoke may be dense, and its mud ultra-muddy, but not any or all of these things can prevent the image of a great city arising before us as a very symbol of civilization."[74] Scrutinizing it in 1835, Tocqueville had been more dialectical: "Here humanity attains its most complete development and its most brutish; here civilization works its miracles, and civilized man is turned back almost into a savage."[75] Like the industrial system which had so accelerated its growth, Manchester was new and, hence, deserving of investigation. Reporting on it in his *Notes of a Tour of the Manufacturing Districts of Lancashire* (1842), W. Cooke Taylor found that the city's poorest were "less known to their wealthy neighbours...than the inhabitants of New Zealand or Kamschata."[76] Generalizing more broadly, he found it "no paradox to assert that the uninstructed operative is worse educated than the uninstructed Indian in the wilds of North America. For my part, I should much rather be exposed to the savages of New Zealand than to a community composed of the worst specimens to be found in the wynds of Glasgow, the cellars of Liverpool, and the Angel-meadows of Manchester."[77] Yet this was very much a matter of "the worst specimens," and, while he feared them, Taylor had enough respect for the industrial workers to conclude that it would be all the more "dreadful...if an element of the worst barbarism were permitted to grow up and develop itself in the midst of the highest civilization."[78] With these workers shielded in part from that dire prospect by Non-Conformist Protestantism, social commentators increasingly turned their attention to London.

The capital fascinated not only the English, but also foreigners, with Flora Tristan's *Promenades dans Londres* (1840) providing inspiration for Sue's *Mystères de Paris* which in turn would be followed by G.W.M. Reynold's *Mysteries of London* (1845-1848). In 1847 the reformer, Ashley, announced his discovery of a distinct "tribe" in London: "their appearance is wild; the matted hair, the disgusting filth...and the barbarian freedom from all superintendence and restraint, fill the mind...with perplexity and dismay."[79] That kind of perception informed Watts Phillips' *The Wild Tribes of London* (1855). Six years later, John Shaw depicted London "slums, inhabited by people so lost to modern morality and civilization...that they may be compared to the wildest colony of savages; transported by an act of conjuration form the centre of Africa."[80] Similar themes would be struck in a series of works by James Greenwood.[81]

Often enough such tracts managed to combine titillation with exhortation. Authors frequently charged that the Churches, so concerned with missionary endeavour abroad, had neglected their duties at home. But the Congregationalist clergyman, Andrew Mearns, could observe in his *Bitter Cry of Outcast London* (1883) that "the churches are making the discovery that seething in the very centre of our great cities, concealed by the thinnest crust of civilization and decency, is a vast amount of moral corruption, of heartbreaking misery and absolute ungodliness."[82] The following year, the founding of the Anglican-sponsored Toynbee Hall testified to such increased interest. Providing a model for religious and secular urban reformers elsewhere, this "settlement house" stood like a pioneer settlement in an urban jungle, some of the savage denizens of which could be saved and/or civilized.

Henry Mayhew's massive *London Labour and the London Poor* (1861-1862) dwarfed all other analyses. Claiming to derive his argument from the anthropologist-psychiatrist, Prichard, and from Sir Andrew Smith, a medical man who in 1826 had been sent by the government to report on Bushman unrest in South Africa, Mayhew asserted:

> Of those millions of human beings that are said to constitute the population of the entire globe, there are—socially, morally, and perhaps even physically considered—but two distinct and broadly marked races,

viz., the wanderers and the settlers—the vagabond and the citizen—the nomadic and the civilized tribes.[83]

Nomadic vices stood opposed to civilized virtues:

> The nomad...is distinguished from the civilized man by repugnance to regular and continuous labour—by his want of providence and laying up a store for the future—by his inability to perceive consequences even slightly removed from his immediate apprehension—by his passion for stupefying herbs and roots, and, when possible, for intoxicating fermented liquors—by his extraordinary powers of enduring privation—by his comparative insensibility to pain—by an immoderate love of gaming, frequently risking his own personal liberty upon a single cast—by the pleasure he experiences in witnessing the suffering of sentient creatures—by his delight in warfare and all perilous sports—by his desire for vengeance—by the looseness of his notions as to property—by the absence of chastity among his women, and his disregard to female honour—and lastly by his vague sense of religion—his rude idea of a Creator, and utter absence of all appreciation of the mercy of the Divine Spirit.[84]

But having presented a catalogue of qualities feared and abhorred by the bourgeoisie, he did not adhere to it rigidly in his finely-detailed and generously-spirited work.

Mayhew shared some themes with other commentators. He presented "the moral and religious state of the London costers" as:

> ...a foul disgrace to us, laughing to scorn our zeal for the 'propagation of the gospel in *foreign* parts', and

> making our many societies for civilization of savages on
> the other side of the globe appear like 'a delusion, a
> mockery, and a snare,' when we have so many people
> sunk in the lowest depths of barbarism around our
> home.[85]

The tone stiffened, however, when Mayhew and his newly-found, more canting collaborators reached the volume devoted to "Those That Will Not Work, comprising Prostitutes, Thieves, Swindlers and Beggars." These "voluntary non-workers" were nothing but "the human parasites of every civilized and barbarian community."[86]

General Booth, the founder of the Salvation Army, shared some of Mayhew's concerns. His *In Darkest England* (1890) followed within a year Henry Stanley's *In Darkest Africa*. If the explorer had presented Africans in racist terms, he still allowed them "the germ...by whose means at some future date civilization may spread."[87] But Stanley's "Darkest Africa" had less to do with the continent's peoples than with the rain forest where the natural processes at work reminded him of "a morning when I went to see the human tide flowing into the city over London Bridge...where I saw the pale, overworked, dwarfed, steep-shouldered on their way to their struggle for existence."[88] Booth picked up on the obsession with the jungle: "In Africa, it is all trees, trees, trees with no other world conceivable; so it is here—it is all vice and poverty and crime."[89] Other parallels were detected: "The foul and fetid breath of our slums," for instance, was "almost as poisonous as that of the African swamp."[90]

Booth, however, was more interested in people than in jungles and swamps. Stanley's chief villains, the Arab slave and ivory traders, resembled nothing so much as "the publicans who flourish on the weakness of our poor."[91] Following up upon the explorer's distinction between "two tribes of savages, the human baboon and the handsome dwarf," Booth found their English counterparts in "the vicious, lazy lout and the toiling slave."[92] Hostile to social exploitation, he still assigned partial responsibility to its victims:

> Just as in Darkest Africa it is only a part of the evil and misery that comes from the superior race who invades the forest to enslave and massacre its miserable inhabitants, so with us, much of the misery of those whose lot we are considering arises from their own habits....A population sodden with drink, steeped in vice, eaten up with every social and physical malady, these are the denizens of Darkest England.[93]

Although he had his own socially disciplinarian ideas about how to change them, conditions seemed to call contemporary civilization into question:

> ...the stony streets of London, if they could only speak, would tell us of tragedies as awful, of ruin as complete, of ravishments as horrible, as if we were in Central Africa, only the ghastly devastation is covered, corpse-like, with the artificialities and hypocrisies of modern civilization.[94]

This militant Christian's equation of civilization and hypocrisy would be echoed by secularists like Mark Twain and Sigmund Freud.

The Quaker philanthropist, Charles Booth, whose *Life and Labour of the People of London* began to appear in 1889, had no such qualms about civilization. He presented the matter in blunt economic terms:

> Every civilization demands the possession of a certain amount of capital, or as the word implies, a quota of

possessions per head. The existing type of what has
been termed 'Western' civilization requires a great
deal of these things, and its advance is based on their
increase.[95]

Consequently, he worried especially about those who relied
upon casual earnings for their support. While no longer
depicted as savages or barbarians, these people still seemed
unable to bear "the regularity and dullness of civilized existence."[96] If the regularity of labour was nothing new in listings
of the features of civilization, the dullness of life, aside from
the scattered comments of a few critics, was distinctly so.

If all the social commentators noted the crime engendered
by poverty, their observations came to be supplemented by
the more specialized studies of the criminologists. In 1827,
Charles Lucas claimed that he had "proven with mathemati-
cal rigor that, with civilization, our persons are more
secure."[97] Even the increasing incidence of crimes against
property could be numbered among the benefits of civilization: it was "among civilized people...merely the result of a
larger development of human freedom."[98] While the sugges-
tion that the development of certain kinds of crimes could be
taken as a measure of civilization would be championed by
others, both persons and property were considered too sacred
in the developing bourgeois order for commentators to be entirely at ease with this argument. It was easy enough to fall
back upon other arguments and images. Thus, in this revealingly titled *Ethnographie des prisons* (1841), J. J. Marquet-Was-
selot claimed: "The convicts are...another people...with its
own habits, instincts, morals."[99]

Intertwined with the dispute over the relationship between crime and civilization was another having to do with
that between crime and mental instability. For Jeremy Bentham, criminals were "forward children, persons of unsound

mind."[100] Striving for balance, Tocqueville maintained that, in the prison population, one encountered those who had been driven to crime through madness and those who had become mad as a result of imprisonment. Few commentators, however, went as far as D.G. Ferrus who, in an effort to carve out a new field for psychiatry, asserted in 1850: "Considered as a whole, criminals are nothing less than madmen."[101] Often enough espoused by physiological determinists, the problem with this approach resided in its apparent denial of the great bourgeois ideal of responsibility.

Physiological determinism, however, seldom constituted an obstacle to moralizing. Among the criminologists, Cesare Lombroso had no difficulty in melding the two currents. Although he tried to respond to his critics by considering the economic, social and political origins of crime in his often revised *Crime: Its Causes and Remedies*, he remained fascinated by his own creation: "born criminals, organically fitted for evil, atavistic reproductions not simply of savage men but even of the fiercest animals."[102] Contending that "many of the characteristics presented by savage races are often found among born criminals," he claimed that his "criminal anthropology" permitted the identification of this kind of criminal through features like "low cranial capacity, retreating forehead...early closing of the cranial *sutures*, the simplicity of the *sutures*...prognathism..anomalies of the ear...relative insensitivity to pain...precocity as to sensual pleasures."[103] He detected parallels between "born criminals" and savages in

...the improvised rules of criminal gangs, the entirely personal influence of the chiefs; the custom of tatooing; the not uncommon cruelty of their games; the excessive use of gestures; the onomatopoeic language with the personification of inanimate things; and a special literature recalling that of heroic times when

73

crimes were celebrated and the thought tended to cloak itself in rhythmic form.[104]

While defending fiercely his notion of the atavistic "born criminal," Lombroso also confronted a problem all too familiar to the criminologists. The increasingly influential study of statistics had revealed a striking paucity of women among the criminal population. That had to be explained. Lombroso turned again to physiology:

> In female animals, in aboriginal women, and in the women of our times, the cerebral cortex…is less active than in the male. The irritation consequent on a degenerative process is therefore neither so constant, nor so lasting, and leads more easily to motor and hysterical epilepsy, or to sexual anomalies than to crime.[105]

Still, some women did become criminals. The potential for female crime was certainly there: "What terrific criminals would children be if they had strong passions, muscular strength and sufficient intelligence and if, moreover, their evil tendencies were exasperated by morbid psychical activity. And women are only big children."[106] Fortunately, in normal circumstances, this potential was "neutralized by piety, maternity, want of passion, sexual coldness, by weakness and undeveloped intelligence."[107] But "born criminals" could also be found among women. Such a creature was literally a monster, "doubly exceptional, as a woman and as a criminal."[108] More generally, while "women are very rarely criminal when compared with men…when criminal they are infinitely worse."[109] This kind of interpretation, applied to the disquieting statistics, raised the question of whether women were or could be full members of civilized society.

Lombroso believed that, while atavistic brutes still stalked that society, civilization had brought change to crime. Increasing its frequency and multiplying its variants, civilization tended to substitute fraud for violence. Social factors had to be considered, and Lombroso quoted approvingly Walter Bagehot: "In order to be persuaded that fineness of feeling diminishes as one descends the social scale, it is not necessary to visit savage peoples; it is enough to talk with the English poor, or even one's own servants."[110] Yet more was at stake in striking the balance in the relationship between civilization and crime. The result was at best mixed. Products of civilization, the steamboat ended piracy, and railways reduced rural banditry. Other inventions and discoveries, as well as modern business techniques, also issued from civilization, but could be directed against it: anarchists, as well as engineers, used dynamite. Some crimes, moreover, benefitted civilization: the Suez Canal, after all, had resulted from "a colossal swindle."[111] If in the end civilization and crime could not be divorced, civilization did hold out, among its multiple blessings, Lombroso's own "criminal anthropology" which promised further advances in "treating the disease."[112]

More than a matter of metaphor, the equation of crime and disease created few difficulties for the criminologists, especially in France where the "medicalization" of crime had come earlier and proceeded faster than elsewhere. Drawing upon the work of psychiatrists in the 1850s, the French elaborated a more flexible variant of determinism in the theory of "degeneration." Whereas Lombroso's "born criminals" had failed to develop beyond an early stage in the evolutionary process, "degenerates" descended from ancestors who had evolved before being plunged into decay by events in their social environment. Familiar to any reader of Zola, such an approach had the advantage of taking into account both environmental and physiological factors: while hereditary organic predisposition might be involved, some triggering event in the external world was needed to produce alcoholism, or insanity, or crime. Swayed by a residual Lamarckianism and the newer Pasteurian bacteriology, the French criminologists attached more importance to social environment than did Lombroso and his school. In doing so, they often followed Gabriel Tarde in emphasizing the importance of imitation in social life.

Contemptuous of Lombroso, Tarde preferred to draw upon the works of French and English psychiatrists for his ideas. An opponent of capital punishment, he sympathized with "the alienist point of view…which shows the criminal is a patient to be cured rather than as a foreign body to be destroyed or eliminated."[113] Still, concerned with the issue of responsibility, he also had reservations: while the mad committed crimes, not every criminal was insane. In this area, whatever his respect for the professionals, he preferred to trust Dostoevsky, "a psychiatrist of great sagacity."[114] Attempting to rescue the notion of individual responsibility from social and physiological determinism, he proposed that "in proportion as a society becomes civilized, should responsibility become individualized."[115] But prescription was not description, and Tarde had problems with contemporary civilization. Rather liking the savages of his day, he denounced imperialism. He also exempted prehistoric savages from charges of wholesale murder and theft, a move which allowed him to strike directly against Lombroso's notion of atavism.

The key problem for this urban-dweller lay in the cities, at once the home of the mob and the heart of civilization. He tried to face the issue squarely: "How…are we to reconcile the improvement of morals which everywhere is the result of civilization with the demoralization aroused by the example of the great cities, the summits and sources of civilization?"[116] His answer lay in positing two stages of civilization:

> A first stage during which inventions and renovating
> initiative flow together haphazard; we have arrived in
> Europe at this stage at the present time. A second stage
> when the afflux becoming exhausted, its elements
> begin to act in concert and have become some sys-
> tem.[117]

Like his younger critic Durkheim, he noted the unhappiness
created by contemporary conditions, but looked forward to a
more socially secure and intellectually cohesive future.

In the meantime, Tarde dwelt in a present where "the
prolonged effect of large cities upon criminality is mani-
fested...in the slow substitution, not exactly of greed for
violence, but of greedy, crafty, and voluptuous violence for
vindictive and brutal violence."[118] Here he confronted those
troubling statistics in regard to women and crime in his own
fashion. If cities had changed the nature of crime, they had
also changed the nature of women, with the latter change, in
turn, influencing crime:

> Unerringly, the slow, universal and perfidious delec-
> tuosity was accomplished under the increasing rule of
> women. We could in some respects represent final
> civilization as the revenge of woman upon man, and
> also the herdsman upon the warrior; of primitive
> tribes, peaceful and oppressed, upon their oppres-
> sors.[119]

Leaving aside the question of what this did to his two-stage
model of civilization, Tarde had managed to produce a vision
of "the return of the repressed" which would have terrified
Freud. But whatever the Frenchman's sympathies for
herdsmen, primitives and perhaps even women, a line had to
be drawn somewhere. Acknowledging the paramount con-

tribution of women to the moralization of the human race, he also contended, in words which Freud would have approved, "There is not a single invention tending toward civilization, however unimportant, which is due to a woman."[120]

The kinds of questions posed by criminologists were already familiar, though in somewhat different terms, to the psychiatrists and again had to do with the relationships between class and/or gender and crime, but, more fundamentally, with those between insanity and civilization. Like the criminologists, the psychiatrists also had to take the findings of statistics into account. Revealing an apparently increasing incidence of insanity or at least an increasing rate of institutionalization of the insane, statistics posed an overlapping series of questions. Did the apparent growth of insanity simply result from a better record-keeping from which the statisticians benefitted? Did the spread of institutionalization simply reflect a greater sensitivity on the part of the public to the presence of the insane? Confronting such questions seriously enough, the psychiatrists steered away from the matter of their own professional stake in the care of the insane and in the discovery or invention of new forms of mental malady. Still, they did have the courage to confront an even larger issue: did the greater complexity of bourgeois society—that is, civilization—accelerate the spread of mental disease?[121]

Drawing upon his expertise as a psychiatrist and an ethnographer, James Cowles Prichard had no doubts about the last matter. He asserted flatly in *A Treatise of Insanity and Other Disorders Affecting the Mind* (1835) that insanity, which hardly existed among the more primitive peoples, characterized civilization. The issue was all the more delicate, for, if such were indeed the case, then those who perceived themselves as genuinely civilized, largely bourgeois males, were most at risk. Hence, Dr. Edgar Sheppard attempted a more nuanced approach to the problem in his *Lectures on Madness in its Medical,*

Legal and Social Aspects (1873): "Apart from the statistical evidence (which is often very untrustworthy), our inclination to one side or another will be much coloured by the meaning which we attach to the conventional term 'civilization.'"[122] But viewing civilization in terms of "wear and tear and high pressure," he favoured the pessimistic side in a debate which had begun even before the word had appeared.[123] Possessed of the word by the end of the eighteenth century, the groundbreaking Philippe Pinel, in his more Rousseauian moments, linked insanity with civilization. His student and successor, Jean Etienne Esquirol, maintained: "Without doubt, civilization occasions diseases, and augments the number of sick, because, by multiplying the means of enjoyment, it causes some to live too well and too fast."[124]

In time, four responses to the question of the relationship between civilization and mental illness appeared. The first reflected the optimistic hopes of the new psychiatrists in regard to their therapeutic skills and techniques. Celebrating the passage in 1838 of a new law regarding insanity, the Parisian *Presse* applauded "civilization repairing the damage it has itself inflicted."[125] The multiplication of asylums and their inhabitants belied such hopes and provoked the second response. By mid-century the American psychiatrist, Edward Jarvis, simply accepted that "insanity is...part of the price we pay for civilization."[126] Several decades later, another American, George M. Beard, provided the third response in celebrating the links between civilization and mental disturbances. Claiming that his neologism "neurasthenia" was a distinctly American malady, he went on to assert that Americans led the way in the march of civilization, a claim soon disputed by Europeans who came to see in the incidence of neurasthenia a more general index of civilization.

The fourth response, which to a greater or lesser degree permeated the others, was the argument that, in civilized conditions, the different classes and genders succumbed to different forms of mental maladies. While different variants of mental disease were constantly being discovered and discarded, the emphasis on aetiology provided a certain degree of continuity in analysis. Seen in class terms, this meant that workers were deemed more likely to come to insanity through alcoholism, members of the bourgeoisie through excessive mental exertion. Seen in gender terms, it meant that males fell victim to the "wear and tear" of external civilization, females to internal physiological forces.

Rather than citing illustrative examples from a voluminous medical literature, it might be better to concentrate on how these issues were presented by the frequently-cited Henry Maudsley (1835-1919). If this Englishman admitted the influence of social environment upon the functioning and malfunctioning of the psyche, his emphasis remained primarily physiological. He believed, like Darwin, that the moral sense had been the last to be acquired by humans in the course of evolution and, pushing the matter beyond Darwin, was the first to disappear in cases of insanity. The dark side of evolution was the possibility of degeneration, with those who had not evolved very far morally and intellectually—like savages and Catholics—finding protection against that prospect. Crime provided a refuge for others. In good Victorian terms there was yet another possibility: "If man could...attain freedom by moderating and controlling the affective or emotional element in his nature, he would vastly lessen the sum of insanity upon earth."[127] While such a condition might lie in the future, the contemporary stage of civilization thwarted its realization.

As for the more specific dispute in regard to civilization and insanity, Maudsley began by accepting the argument that the former accelerated the incidence of the latter. But in 1872 he acknowledged: "It may...be safely said that there is scarcely a single theoretical argument in favour of the alleged increase of insanity which may not be met with as strong a theoretical argument on the other side."[128] Five years later, secure in his lucrative private practice, he had made up his mind:

> First...there is no evidence of an increased production of insanity among the non-pauper class, and, secondly...the undoubted increase of admissions into pauper asylums is to be attributed mainly to the successive regulations by which persons have been steadily forced into asylums..[129]

But forced admissions did not exhaust the class factor, for paupers were more at risk, as were agricultural rather than urban workers. As for the middle class, Maudsley provided his bourgeois readers with the standard advice that, rather than psychically bankrupt themselves, they should husband their psychic capital.

Involving himself in another dispute, he accepted the statistics which indicated that female lunatics out-numbered their male counterparts. But he explained that not only were female lunatics subject to a greater number of relapses than males, but, more importantly, they tended to outlive the males. In the interest of greater accuracy, he also dismissed the notion that "governesses were victims out of all proportion to their numbers."[130] Arguing that it had "not been settled definitely, whether more men than women go mad," he introduced a distinction already made by others: "Men are exposed to more numerous and powerful extrinsic causes, and women, by virtue of their sexual organization, to more numerous and powerful intrinsic causes of insanity."[131] Himself oriented primarily to internal causation, he could be as blunt as any French psychiatrist: "The ecstatic trances of such saintly women as Catherine of Siena and St. Theresa...were, though they knew it not, little else than vicarious sexual orgasms."[132] But he could also be quite conventional: diseases of the uterus influenced the brain. He did acknowledge, however, that "while without a doubt hysterical symptoms sometimes run by degrees into actual insanity...considering how common a disease hysteria is, it must be confessed that this is rare."[133]

Receiving its most interesting treatment in Robert B. Carter's *On the Pathology of Hysteria* (1853), this condition fascinated nineteenth-century medical men. Carter linked it to sexual repression which, in turn, was linked to civilization:

> For while the advance of civilization and its ever-increasing complications of social intercourse tend to call forth new feelings, and by their means throw amativeness into the shade as one powerful emotion among others; still its absolute intensity is in no way lessened, and from the modern necessity for its entire concealment, it is likely to produce hysteria in a large number of women subject to its influence, than it would do if the state of society permitted its free expression.[134]

While he allowed for female sexuality and recognized the existence of male hysterics, Carter accepted the conventional distinction between the feeling woman and the thinking man. Several decades later the great Jean-Martin Charcot also accepted male hysteria, but continued to believe that the most numerous sufferers were female, a view which led a feminist to accuse him in 1888 of "a sort of vivisection of women under the pretext of studying a disease for which he knows neither the cause nor the treatment."[135] But when it came to female sexuality, vivisection was not solely a matter of metaphor. Clitoridectomies did take place, and criminologist, Hans Gross, quoted approvingly an Austrian surgeon who was supposed to have remarked that he experimented with new operative techniques on women because "they are less subject to pain, for like savages, they are beings of a lower status and hence better able to resist pain than men."[136]

The most obvious pain experienced by women was that of child-birth, but even for the Victorian "angel in the house," it was only a part of the larger cycle of menstruation, pregnancy, and menopause. That pattern seemed to embed women in Nature in a much more immediate fashion than men. Female sexuality, however, did not necessarily imply female sexual pleasure. For the Victorian expert on prostitution, Dr. William Acton, "Strong passions, save in exceptional cases at certain times, and in advanced stages of dissipation, as little disturb the economy of the human as they do that of the female brute."[137] Accepting prostitution as "an inevitable attendant upon civilized, and especially close-packed population," he urged the English to follow the example of France, "the country that has always led the way in the advance of modern civilization," and "to create and maintain a class of harlots for the benefit of public health."[138]

While contrasted with bourgeois domesticity, prostitution also served as its complement. As the historian, William Lecky, put the matter in 1869, "Herself the supreme type of vice, she is ultimately the most efficient guardian of virtue. But for her the unchallenged purity of countless happy homes would be polluted."[139] A few years earlier, Mayhew and a collaborator had brought vice and virtue together in a more evolutionary fashion:

> The prostitute class, as we proceed from the savage to the highest point of civilization, becomes more conspicuous because more isolated. This is accompanied by another process, which is a superior standard to

measure the social evolution of a people. Women respect themselves as men respect them. Where locks and bolts, scourges and cudgels, are the guarantees of female chastity, it is only preserved where there is no opportunity to lose it. When the protecting influence springs from within, the women moves a virtuous being, defended even from a licentious glance by the impenetrable cloud which her native modesty and virtue diffuse around her.[140]

Obviously, London, with its conspicuous prostitutes and virtuous women, was a highly civilized city.

Clearly, prostitutes were not perceived as "normal" women, but it was even a question as to whether any such women existed. The American physician, Silas Weir Mitchell, observed in 1888: "The man who does not know sick women does not know women."[141] The more usual view, however, came from Tarde. While agreeing with Comte in regard to woman's moralizing force within society, he went on to portray her as "a rebel against every civilizing influence."[142] For Tarde, as for many of his contemporaries, woman was such a force without herself being capable of becoming fully civilized. This conviction had its own logic: Civilization rested on distance from and control over Nature; woman's reproductive system immersed her in Nature; *ergo*, woman was less able than man to reach that degree of civilization which stood at the end of a long evolutionary process. Darwin both codified pre-existing sentiment and lent his prestige to it when he proclaimed that "it is generally admitted that with woman the powers of perception, and perhaps of imitation, are more strongly marked than in men; but some, at least, of these faculties are characteristic of the lower races, and therefore of a past and lower state of civilization."[143] Whatever his doubts as to what might ultimately be accomplished, he did at least urge the improvement of her mental condition.

Writing shortly after the American emancipation of the slaves, Darwin's follower, Thomas Henry Huxley, turned his attention to "the 'irresistible' woman question."[144] He championed more and better education for women. Indeed, he went farther: "Let the women who feel inclined...descend into the gladiatorial arena of life....Let them, if they so please, become barristers, politicians."[145] Impressive words, but he believed that Nature would render judgment: "The big chests, the massive brains, the vigourous muscles and stout frames of the best of men will carry the day, whenever it is worth their while to contest the prizes of life with the best women."[146] The other side of the coin was just as distinctly physiological—the imperatives of motherhood.[147] But even efforts at more balanced presentations revealed the power of stereotypes. Thus, having largely neglected women in his *History of Civilization in England*, Henry Buckle tried to do them justice in "The Influence of Women on the Progress of Knowledge" where he tried to link the increasing influence of women, the growth of knowledge, and the development of civilization. Intending it as praise for women, he still argued that "women possess more of what is called intuition. They cannot see as far as man can, but what they do see they see quicker."[148]

Perhaps surer of what civilization was about—or at least who it was about—Frenchmen still did not go untroubled by the demands of women.[149] The matter was further complicated in France by the not entirely unfounded conviction on the part of the republicans that providing votes for women would increase the clerical influence in political life. At the turn of the century, the republican sociologist-ideologue, Emile Durkheim, had to confront such matters. Hardly a romantic, this positivist-functionalist defined marriage as "a regulation of sexual relations, including not only the physical instincts which this intercourse involves, but the feelings of every sort gradually engrafted by civilization on the foundation of physical desire."[150] Males had been both the primary beneficiaries and victims of the civilizing process. As she remained closer to Nature, "Woman's sexual needs have less of a mental character because, generally speaking, her mental life is less developed....Being a more instinctive creature than is man, woman has only to follow her instincts to find calmness and peace."[151] Behind that distinction lay such concrete matters as suicide, the double standard, divorce, and demands for changes in the relations between the genders.

The gradualist, Emile Durkheim, felt compelled to draw a line:

> As for the champions today of equal rights for woman with those of man, they forget that the work of centuries cannot be instantly abolished; that juridical equality cannot be legitimate so long as the psychological inequality is so flagrant. Our efforts must be to reduce the latter. For man and woman to be equally protected by the same institution they must first of all be creatures of the same nature.[152]

Reformism gave way to condescension:

> ...man is more thoroughly socialized than woman. His aspirations and humour have in large part a collective origin, while his companion's are more directly influenced by her organism....To be sure, we have no reason to suppose that woman may ever be able to fulfil the same functions in society as man, but she will be able to play a part in society which, while peculiarly her own, may yet be more active and important than that of today. The female sex will not again become

similar to the male; on the contrary, we may foresee
that it will become more different. But these differences will become of greater social use than in the past.[153]

He queried: "Why...should not aesthetic functions become
woman's as man, more and more absorbed by functions of
utility, has to renounce them?"[154]

Durkheim's views appear to be those of a stuffy academic
mandarin when compared to those of Havelock Ellis. On a
host of issues—the sexual feelings of women, the sexual ignorance of men, the right of both genders to sexual pleasure,
the possibility of bisexuality, sympathy towards homo-
sexuality and nudism—this Englishman seemed to be the complete antithesis of the Victorians. In fact, he more often
re-worked rather than trans-valued nineteenth-century shibboleths. One finds this, for instance, in his argument that:

> ...men possess a greater power of foresight and self-
> control than women....The sexual sphere is immense-
> ly larger in woman, so that when its activity is once
> aroused it is much more difficult to master or con-
> trol....It is, therefore, unfair to women, and unduly
> favours men, when too heavy a premium is placed on
> foresight and control.[155]

Nor could the Darwinian element be escaped: "The masculine
tendency to delight in domination, the feminine tendency to
delight in submission, still maintain the ancient tradition
when the male pursued the female."[156]

Nevertheless, Ellis detected a "well-marked tendency with
civilization to the abolition of sexual difference."[157] He linked
this tendency to economic changes which had produced the
"New Woman" who claimed the right to support herself and to
make moral, including sexual, choices of her own. If he cham-

pioned such moral responsibility, the fruit of economic independence, he still doubted the achievement of full economic equality with males, for "the special process by which the race is propagated demands a much greater expenditure of time and energy on the part of women than of men."[158] Going beyond biological constraints, this great sexual emancipator celebrated maternity just as much as any Victorian moralist. Indeed, perhaps realizing just how close he had come to the Victorian distinction between the male public and the female private spheres, he had to specify: "It should scarcely be necessary to say that to assert that motherhood is a woman's supreme function is by no means to assert that her activities should be confined to the home."[159] This qualification, however, did not divert him from a far more conventional opinion: "As long as women are distinguished from men by primary sexual characters—so long as they conceive and bear—so long will they remain unequal to men in the highest psychic processes."[160]

Americans eager to escape their own variety of Victorianism greeted Ellis as a liberator. Such was the case with the psychologist, G. Stanley Hall, who enthused: "The *vita sexualis* is normally a magnificent symphony, the rich and varied orchestration of which brings the individual in the closest *rapport* with the life of the great Biologos."[161] Still, while presenting himself as a progressive psychologist and educator, he proved himself to be more explicitly conservative than Ellis when it came to the "New Woman" and, indeed, women more generally. He tried to buttress this conservatism with the most up-to-date information; thus, referring to Breuer and Freud's *Studies in Hysteria* (1895), he noted: "A sad new light upon the peculiar vulnerability of early adolescence in girls is presented in a recent minute study of eighteen cases of hysteria in highly cultivated subjects."[162] But in his view, even if she managed to escape the threats of adolescence, a woman was bound to encounter further problems:

The normal woman in her prime, no matter how healthy, is more sensitive, more prone to depression, ex-
citable, moody, feels more fatigued, distracted, suffers
pain more or less intense in different parts of her body,
especially in the head, is more liable to discontent,
quarrelsomeness, unstable in appetite and sleep, disappointed, feels oppressed and can do less work with
her mind and body.[163]

Although he admitted that little was known about menstruation, he did not hesitate to ascribe these disabilities to it. Still,
whatever her physical and mental defects, woman as mother
emerged as a civilizing force: "The soul of the normal
mother...turns toward the child and toward the future, and
the father, whom she originally reclaimed from a feral, roving
lover, later follows."[164]

The reactionary Gustave Le Bon would surely have
regarded the sentiments of an Ellis or a Hall as claptrap. His
view of women was forthright enough:

In the most intelligent races, as among the Parisians, there
are a large number of women whose brains are closer in
size to those of gorillas than to the most developed male
brains....All psychologists who have studied the intelligence of women, as well as poets and novelists, recognize today that they represent the most inferior forms of
human evolution and that they are closer to children and
savages than to adult civilized man. They excel in fickle-
ness, inconstancy, absence of thought and logic, and in-
capacity to reason. Without doubt there are some
distinguished women, very superior to the average man,
but they are as exceptional as the birth of any monstrosity,
as, for example, of a gorilla with two heads; consequently,
we may neglect them entirely.[165]

Emancipation of any sort was not on his agenda.

If women fared worst, Le Bon did not neglect other groups which have been considered here. He had no use for the savage in the past or present: the pre-historical savage was "an ignorant and ferocious brute, as ignorant as the modern savage of goodness, morality and pity."[166] A proponent of "association" rather than "assimilation" in the colonial sphere, he explained that "one of the principal reasons for our inability to impose our civilization upon inferior peoples can be expressed briefly: It is too complicated for them."[167] Yet he preferred African rulers to the socialists who terrified him. He charged that, "reverting to primitive instincts, the mentality of the modern worker is becoming that of a barbarian."[168] It was not simply a matter of reversion, but also of a failure in evolution: "An advanced civilization retains all the residue of the successive stages through which it passed. The cave and Attila's barbarians still have their representatives among us."[169] Directing his venom against a variety of groups, he argued:

> All civilized societies drag behind them a residue of degenerates. Vagabonds, beggars, fugitives from justice, thieves, assassins, and starving creatures that live from day to day....In ordinary times these waste products of civilization are more or less restrained by the police. During revolution nothing restrains them and they can easily gratify their instincts to murder and plunder.[170]

Perceived in these terms, revolution constituted the fundamental threat to civilization.

Le Bon drew all these images together in his most famous work, *Psychologie des foules* (1895). By participating in a crowd, "man...descends several degrees in the scale of civilization."[171]

While he acknowledged that crowds could act morally, he insisted:

> Several of the special characteristics of crowds, such as impulsiveness, irritability at reasoning, the absence of judgment and of civilized spirit, the exaggeration of sentiments, and yet others, can be observed also among beings belonging to inferior forms of evolution, like the savage and the child.[172]

Put more pithily, "The crowd is not only impulsive and fickle. Like the savage, it permits no obstacle between its desire and the realization of this desire."[173] Crowds fundamentally resembled each other and yet differed along racial lines: "Crowds are above all feminine, but the most feminine of all are Latin crowds."[174] Still, whatever his scorn for the masses, Le Bon stood ready to advise those interested in manipulating them: "The true leader of men begins by seducing, and the seduced being, a crowd or woman, has only one opinion, that of the seducer, only one will, his."[175]

Defined as "the elimination of the instinctive by the rational," civilization provided the standard for such judgments.[176] Given the role which he assigned to people like himself, he had no problems with it: "Created by an elite, civilization can progress only by it."[177] This conviction entailed a corollary: "Great civilizations prospered only by knowing how to dominate their inferior elements."[178] Torn between contempt and terror, Le Bon had no doubts as to who constituted those elements in his world: the savages abroad and the savage workers, criminals, lunatics and women at home, with the domestic savages at their most dangerous when collected in crowds. While brought together in a more coherent fashion, none of this, not even the depiction of the crowd, was especially new. It is then all the more significant that Freud should refer approvingly to Le Bon's "deservedly famous" *Psychologie des foules*. Then again, Freud had his own interest in civilization.

NOTES

1. Herbert Spencer, *The Principles of Psychology*, I (Boston: Longwood Press, 1977), p. 581.
2. Quoted in George W. Stocking, Jr., *Race, Culture, and Evolution: Essays in the History of Anthropology* (New York: The Free Press, 1968), p. 25.
3. Jean-Marc-Gaspard Itard, *The Wild Boy of Aveyron (Rapports et mémoires sur le sauvage de l'Aveyron)* (New York: The Century Co., 1932), pp. xxi-xxii.
4. *Ibid.*, p. 50.
5. *Ibid.*, p. 93.
6. Quoted in Cohen, *The French Encounter* , p. 237.
7. Quoted in Stephen J. Gould, *The Mismeasure of Man* (New York: W. W. Norton, 1981), p. 84.
8. James Cowles Prichard, *Researches into the Physical History of Man* (Chicago: University of Chicago Press, 1973), pp. 236-37.
9 . *Ibid.*, pp. 223, 209. The view of civilization as domestication would have consequences for both men and women, but especially for women.
10. Quoted in George W. Stocking, Jr., *Victorian Anthropology* (New York: Free Press, 1987), p. 218.
11. *Ibid.*
12. *Ibid.*, p. 69.
13. Tylor, *Origins of Culture*, I, p. 43.
14. *Ibid.*, pp. 31, 315.
15. Charles Darwin, *The Voyage of the Beagle* (New York: Bantam Books, 1958), p. 176.
16. *Ibid.*, p. 376.
17. Darwin, "The Descent of Man," pp. 541, 543.
18. *Ibid.*, p. 505.
19. *Ibid.*, p. 501.
20. *Ibid.*, p. 504.
21. Alfred R. Wallace, *The Malay Archipelago* (London: Macmillan and Co., 1922), p. 70.
22. *Ibid.*, p. 198

23. *And thus these people pass their simple lives,*
     They are a peaceful race; few serious crimes
     Are known among them; they not (sic) rob nor murder
     And all the complicated villanies
     Of men called civilized are here unknown.
     Alfred Wallace, *A Narrative of Travels on the Amazon and Rio Negro* (London: War, Lock & Bowdin, 1895), p. 176.
24. Wallace, *Malay Archipelago*, p. 457.
25. *Ibid.*, p. 456.
26. Lewis Henry Morgan, *Ancient Society or Researches in the Lines of Human Progress From Savagery Through Barbarism To Civilization.* (Cleveland: Meridian Books, 1963), p. 526.
27. *Ibid.*, p. 537.
28. *Ibid.*, p. 569.
29. Quoted in Christine Bolt, *Victorian Attitudes to Race* (London: Routledge & Kegan Paul, 1971), p.145.
30. Quoted in David Gasman, *The Scientific Origin of National Socialism: Social Darwinism in Ernst Haekel and the German Monist League* (London: Macdonald, 1971), p. 390.
31. Eduard von Hartmann, *Philosophy of the Unconscious. Speculative Results According to the Inductive Method of Psychical Science*, II (London: Kegan Paul, Trench, Trüber & Co., 1931), p. 12.
32. A French journalist explained in 1864: "It is a fatal law that the inferior races will disappear in the face of the superior ones." Two years later the *Popular Magazine of Anthropology* had it: " to colonize and to extirpate are synonymous terms." Quoted in Cohen, *French Encounter*, p. 249, and Bolt, *Victorian Attitudes*, p. 20. For American views, see below.
33. Quoted in Douglas A. Lorimer, *Colour, Class and the Victorians: English Attitudes to the Negro in the mid-Nineteenth Century* (Leicester: Leicester University Press, 1978), p.76.
34. Quoted in Kiernan, *Lords of Human Kind*, p. 277.
35. Quoted in H. Alan Cairns, *Prelude to Imperialism: British Reactions to Central African Society, 1840-1890* (London: Routledge & Kegan Paul, 1965), p. 92.
36. To Arthur Tidman, May 23, 1856, I. Schapera (ed.), *Livingstone's Missionary Correspondence, 1841-1856* (Berkeley: University of California Press, 1981), pp. 306-12, 307-08.
37. Mary Kingsley, *Travels in West Africa* (London: Frank Cass & Co., 1965), pp. 663-64. Still, her cheerful comparison of the Africans with the Irish might give one pause.
38. *Ibid.*, p. 680,
39. Quoted in Pearce, *Savages of America*, p. 5.
40. "Letter from the Secretary of War Transmitting a Report of the progress which has been made in the Civilization of the Indian Tribes," Jan. 17,

1820. Thomas Cochrane (ed.), *The New American State Papers: Indian Affairs: General*, II (Washington: Scholarly Resources, 1972), p. 576.

41. "Letter from Thomas L. McKenny to James Barbour," Dec. 13, 1825, *Ibid.*, pp. 675-81. p. 676; T. Hartley Crawford, "Report of the Commissioner of Indian Affairs," Nov. 25, 1844. *Ibid.*, pp. 86-118, p. 94. William Medell, "Report of the Commissioner of Indian Affairs, Nov. 24, 1845, *Ibid.*, p. 125.

42. George Catlin, *North American Indians* (London: Penguin Books, 1989), p. 47.

43. *Ibid.*, p. 526.

44. Horace Greeley, *An Overland Journey from New York to San Francisco*, excerpted in Nancy B. Black and Bette S. Wiedman (eds.), *White on Red: Images of the American Indian* (Port Washington: Kennikat Press, 1976), p. 258.

45. Quoted in Brian W. Dippie, *The Vanishing American. White Attitudes and U.S. Indian Policy* (Middletown: Wesleyan University Press, 1982), p. 87.

46. Quoted in Horseman, *Race and Manifest Destiny*, p. 273.

47. *Ibid.*, p. 155.

48. Quoted in Robert M. Utley, *The Indian Frontier of the American West, 1846-1890* (Albuquerque: University of New Mexico Press, 1984), p. 51.

49. Quoted in Leonard Dinnirstein, Roger Nicols, and David M. Reimers, *Natives and Strangers: Ethnic Groups and the Building of America* (New York: Oxford University Press, 1979), p. 200.

50. Quoted in Utley, *Indian Frontier*, p. 219.

51. Quoted in Drinnon, *Facing West*, p. 508.

52. Quoted in Pearce, *Savages of America*, pp. 208-09.

53. Quoted in Eugen Weber, *Peasants into Frenchmen. The Modernization of Rural France* (Stanford: Stanford University Press, 1976), p. 3.

54. Quoted in Pierre Michel, *Les Barbares, 1789-1848: Un mythe romantique* (Lyon: Presses universitaires de Lyon, 1961), p. 379.

55. Quoted in Louis Chevalier, *Laboring Classes and Dangerous Classes in Paris During the First Half of the Nineteenth Century* (Princeton: Princeton University Press, 1973), pp. 403-04.

56. Jules Michelet, *The People* (Urbana: University of Illinois Press, 1973), p. 105. The peasantry usually fared better than urban artisans and workers. Michelet presented peasants as "not only the most numerous part of the nation but also the strongest, the healthiest and the best." *Ibid.*, p. 35. For the liberal poet-politician, Lamartine, "It is not only grain which springs from the cultivated earth, it is an entire civilization." In his view, peasants stood in welcome contrast to urban worker, "subject to the passions of profusion and the passions of misery." Quoted in Michel, *Barbares*, p. 304. Conservatives especially championed such views.

57. Quoted in Weber, *Peasants*, p. 4.

58. Edmond de Goncourt, *Journal*, Sept. 6, 1870, excerpted in Roland Stromberg, (ed.), *Realism, Naturalism, and Symbolism: Modes of Thought and Expression in Europe, 1848-1914* (New York: Harper & Row, 1968), pp. 72-91, p. 74.

59. He depicted the silk manufacturers of Lyon living, like "colonial planters in the midst of their slaves," under the constant threat of "a kind of insurrection along the lines of Saint-Dominique." Quoted in Michel, *Barbares* pp. 210, 214.

60. Quoted in *Ibid.*, pp. 221, 222.

61. Quoted in *Ibid.*, p. 237.

62. Quoted in *Ibid.*, p. 232.

63. Quoted in *Ibid.*

64. March 28, 1871, Stromberg (ed.), *Realism, Naturalism and Symbolism*, p. 82.

65. Maxime du Camp, *Les convulsions de Paris*, IV, *La commune a l'Hotel de Ville* (Paris: Hachette, 1881).

66. *Ibid.*, p. 50.

67. Quoted in Chevalier, *Laboring Classes*, p. 144.

68. Quoted in *Ibid.*, p. 360.

69. Quoted in *Ibid.*

70. Quoted in *Ibid.*, p. 359.

71. Quoted in *Ibid.*

72. Quoted in Gertrude Himmelfarb, *The Idea of Poverty: England in the Early Industrial Age* (New York: Alfred A. Knopf, 1989), p. 492.

73. Quoted in Asa Briggs, *Victorian Cities* (Harmondsworth: Penguin Books, 1968), p. 64.

74. Quoted in *Ibid.*, p. 74.

75. de Tocqueville, *Journeys to England and Ireland*, in Hervie, Martin and Scharf (eds.), *Industrialisation and Culture, 1830-1914*, p. 42.

76. W. Cooke Taylor, *Notes of a Tour of the Manufacturing Districts of Lancashire* (London: Frank Cass and Co., 1968), pp. 13-14.

77. *Ibid.*, p. 128.

78. *Ibid.*, p. 129.

79. Quoted in Himmelfarb, *Idea of Poverty*, pp. 275-76.

80. Andrew Lees, *Cities Perceived: Urban Society in European and American Thought, 1820-1940)* (New York: Columbia University Press, 1985), p. 28.

81. *The Seven Curses of London* (1869), *In Strange Company* (1873), *The Wilds of London* (1874), and *Low Life Deeps* (1876).

82. Quoted in Garth Stedman Jones, *Outcast London: A Study of the Relationship of Classes in Victorian Society* (Oxford: The Clarendon Press, 1971), p. 222.

83. Henry Mayhew, *London Labour and the London Poor*, I (New York: Dover Publications, 1968), p. 1.

84. *Ibid.*, p. 2.

85. *Ibid.*, p. 101.
86. *Ibid.*, IV, p. 31.
87. Henry M. Stanley, *In Darkest Africa or the Quest, Rescue and Retreat of Emin, Governor of Equatoria*, I (London: Sampson, Low, Marston, Seark, and Remington, 1890), pp. 91-92.
88. *Ibid.*, II, p. 79.
89. General Booth, *In Darkest England and the Way Out* (London: International Headquarters of the Salvation Army, 1890), p. 12.
90. *Ibid.*
91. *Ibid.*
92. *Ibid.*
93. *Ibid.*, pp. 13-14.
94. *Ibid.*, p. 13.
95. Alfred Fried and Richard Elman (eds.), *Charles Booth's London: A Portrait of the Poor at the Turn of the Century, Drawn from his "Life and Labour of the People of London."* (London: Hitchinson, 1969), p. 280.
96. *Ibid.*, p. 14.
97. Quoted in André Normandeau, "Charles Lucas (1803-1850)," Hermann Mannheim (ed.), *Pioneers in Criminology* (Montclair: Patterson Smith, 1977), pp. 138-57, p. 152.
98. *Ibid.*, p. 153.
99. Quoted in Michel Foucault, *Discipline and Punish: The Birth of the Prison* (New York: Vintage Books, 1977) p. 253.
100. Quoted in Michael Ignatieff, *A Just Measure of Pain: The Penitentiary in the Industrial Revolution, 1750-1850* (London: Penguin Books, 1989), p. 66.
101. Quoted in Foucault, *Discipline*, p. 254.
102. Cesare Lombroso, *Crime: Its Causes and Remedies* (Boston: Little, Brown and Company, 1911), p. 428.
103. *Ibid.*, pp. 365-66.
104. *Ibid.*, p. 366.
105. Cesare Lombroso and William Ferro, *The Female Offender* (New York: Appleton, 1897), p.111.
106. *Ibid.*, p. 151.
107. *Ibid.*
108. *Ibid.*, pp. 151-52.
109. *Ibid.*, p. 288.
110. Lombroso, *Crime*, p. 52.
111. *Ibid.*, p. 443.
112. *Ibid.*, p. 58.
113. Gabriel Tarde, *Penal Philosophy* (Boston: Little, Brown and Co., 1912), p. 111.
114. *Ibid.*, p. 229.
115. *Ibid.*, p. 148.
116. *Ibid.*, p. 549

117. *Ibid.*, p. 392.
118. *Ibid.*, p. 359. He observed that in cities "a despair caused by the consequences of debauchery or gambling, by some financial catastrophe, is sometimes sufficient to plunge a civilized Frenchman into a loss of class, that jungle of civilization." *Ibid.*, p. 272.
119. *Ibid.*, p. 6.
120. *Ibid.*, fn. 1, p. 6. Largely jettisoning the moralization element, Freud argued in 1932: "It seems that women have made few contributions to the discoveries and inventions in the history of civilization." Sigmund Freud, *New Introductory Lectures* (New York: W. W. Norton & Co., 1965), p. 117.
121. Although the matter cannot be pursued here, suicide posed somewhat similar problems. See Thomas G. Masaryk, *Suicide and the Meaning of Civilization* (Chicago: University of Chicago Press, 1970) and Emile Durkheim, *Suicide: A Study in Sociology* (New York: The Free Press, 1951).
122. Quoted in George Rosen, *Madness in Society: Chapters in the Historical Sociology of Mental Illness* (New York: Harper Torchbooks, 1969), p. 189. The sixth chapter of Rosen's book provides an excellent summation of the Anglo-American treatments of the madness-civilization issue. Despite the English title given to Michel Foucault's *Histoire de la folie à l'âge classique*, he did little with the matter in *Madness and Civilization*. This is understandable in that the term "civilization" appeared late in the period with which he was concerned. What is less understandable is the relative lack of attention paid to the issue by historians of nineteenth-century French psychiatry.
123. *Ibid.*
124. Jean Etienne Equerol, *Mental Maladies: A Treatise on Insanity*, excerpted in Charles Goshen (ed.), *A Documentary History of Psychiatry: A Source Book on Historical Principles* (London: Vision Press, 1967), pp. 315-69, p. 350.
125. Quoted in Jan Goldstein, *Console and Classify: The French Psychiatric Profession in the Nineteenth Century* (Cambridge: Cambridge University Press, 1987), p. 319.
126. Quoted in Rosen, *Madness*, p. 391.
127. Henry Maudsley, *The Pathology of Mind* (London: Macmillan & Co., 1879), p. 299.
128. Quoted in Michael Collie, *Henry Maudsley, Victorian Psychiatrist: A Bibliographical Study* (Winchester: St. Paul's Bibliographies, 1988), p. 102.
129. Quoted in *Ibid.*, p. 157.
130. Henry Maudsley, *Responsibility in Mental Diseases* (London: Kegan Paul, Trench, Trüber & Co., 1892), p. 169. He argued that this belief had arisen from the disproportionate number of governesses admitted to a single hospital, Bethlehem, where the very conditions of admission accounted for the phenomenon. Still, given the conditions of life of

governesses in the nineteenth century, a disproportionate incidence of
insanity might well have marked their profession.

131. *Ibid.*, pp. 166-67.
132. Ibid., pp. 143-44.
133. *Ibid.*, p. 463.
134. Quoted in Ilsa Veith, *Hysteria: The History of a Disease* (Chicago: University of Chicago Press, 1965), p. 202.
135. Quoted in Goldstein, *Console*, p. 375.
136. Hans Gross, *Criminal Psychology: A Manual for Judges, Practitioners, and Students* (Boston: Little, Brown and Co., 1911), p. 362.
137. William Acton, *Prostitution* (New York: Frederick Praeger, 1968), p. 127.
138. *Ibid.*, pp. 32, 97, 111.
139. William E. A. Lecky, *History of European Morals from Augustus to Charlemange*, I (New York: George Brazillier, 1955), p. 283. Derived from Christianity, the association of prostitution and pollution received a more scientistic gloss in Alexandre Parent-Duchâtelet's *De la prostitution dans la ville de Paris* (1836). Having established his reputation on the basis of studies of the Parisian sewer system, he had no difficulty in turning to prostitution: "If, without scandalizing anyone, I was able to enter the sewers, handle putrid matter, spend part of my time in the refuse pits, and live as it were in the midst of the most abject and disgusting products of human congregations, why should I blush to tackle a sewer of another kind (more unspeakably foul, I admit, than all the others) in the well-grounded hope of effecting some good by examining all the facets it may offer?" Quoted in Charles Bernheimer, *Figures of Ill Repute: Representing Prostitution in Nineteenth-Century France* (Cambridge: Harvard University Press, 1989), p. 15.
140. Henry Mayhew, *London*, IV, pp. 57-58.
141. Quoted in Elaine Showalter, "Victorian Women and Insanity," Andrew Scull (ed.), *Madness, Mad-Doctors and Madmen: The Social History of Psychiatry in the Victorian Era* (Philadelphia: University of Pennsylvania Press, 1981), pp. 313-38, p. 330.
142. Tarde, *Penal Philosophy*, p. 5.
143. Darwin, "Descent of Man," p. 873.
144. "Emancipation—Black and White," Thomas Henry Huxley, *Lay Sermons, Addresses and Reviews* (New York: D. Appleton & Co., 1871), pp. 20-26, p. 22.
145. *Ibid.*, p. 25.
146. *Ibid.*
147. Again stressing the importance of the reproductive function, Maudsley argued in "Sex in Mind and Education" (1874) that women who sought participation in a man's world, as well as the education which would prepare them for it, would inevitably fall short of womanly ideals. Given Maudsley's contempt for savages, Dr. Elizabeth Garrett Anderson's reply carried, in the context of the day, a

deadly twist of its own, for she charged the distinguished psychiatrist with being an "Ashanti warrior" whose calls for restrictive policies, "whether as applied to negroes, agricultural labourers or women" brought to mind the "miscellaneous and obsolete projectiles" used by Africans in their efforts to halt the advance of civilization. Quoted in Collie, *Maudsley*, p. 51.

148. "The Influence of Women and the Progress of Knowledge," Henry Thomas Buckle, *Essays* (New York: S. Appleton & Co., 1863), p. 180.
149. Neither did the Central Europeans, but given their distinction between Culture and Civilization, they spent less time relating women to civilization than in relating neurasthenia to it.
150. Durkheim, *Suicide*, p. 270.
151. *Ibid.*, p. 272.
152. *Ibid.*, p. 386.
153. *Ibid.*, p. 385.
154. *Ibid.*, Across the Rhine, Georg Simmel would pursue this line of thought with far greater sophistication and empathy. See Georg Simmel, *On Women, Sexuality and Love* (New Haven: Yale University Press, 1984).
155. Havelock Ellis, *Studies in the Psychology of Sex*, II, *Part III: Sex in Relation to Society* (New York: Random House, 1936), p. 174.
156. Havelock Ellis, *Studies*, I, *Part III: Sexual Selection in Man* (New York: Random House, 1942), p. 174.
157. *Ibid.*
158. Ellis, *Studies*, II, *III*, p. 410.
159. *Ibid.*, fn. 1, p. 3.
160. Quoted in Iwan Bloch, *The Sexual Life of Our Time in Its Relations to Modern Civilization* (New York: Allied Book Co., 1926), p. 72.
161. G. Stanley Hall, *Adolescence: Of Psychology and Its Relations to Physiology, Anthropology, Sociology, Sex, Crime, Religion and Education* I (New York: Arno Press and the New York Times, 1969), p. 43.
162. *Ibid.*, II, p. 121.
163. *Ibid.*, I, p. 492.
164. *Ibid.*, II, p. 125.
165. Quoted in Gould, *Mismeasure of Man*, pp. 105-105.
166. Gustave Le Bon, *The French Revolution and the Psychology of Revolution* (New Brunswick: Transaction Books, 1980), p. 159.
167. Gustave Le Bon, *La Psychologie politique et la Défense sociale* (Paris: Ernst Flammarion, n.d.), p. 271.
168. *Ibid.*, p. 363.
169. "Aphorismes du Temps Présent," excerpted in Alice Widener (ed.), *Gustave Le Bon: The Man and His Works* (Indianapolis: Liberty Press, 1979), pp. 267-306, p. 279.
170. Gustave Le Bon, *French Revolution*, p. 99.

171. Gustave Le Bon, *Psychologie des foules* (Paris: Presses universitaires de France, 1963), p. 14.
172. *Ibid.*, pp. 16-17.
173. *Ibid.*, p. 18.
174. *Ibid.*
175. Le Bon, *Psychologie Politique*, p. 137.
176. *Ibid.*, p. 223.
177. Widener (ed.), *Le Bon* p. 288.
178. *Ibid.*, p. 289.

3

FREUD

SIGMUND FREUD, at his most enlightened, derided the Germanic distinction between culture and civilization, a distinction which in his lifetime often served as a cloak for anti-Semitism. He used both terms interchangeably. If anything, his preference lay with civilization, perhaps a sign of his identification with Western rather than Central European tradition. Be that as it may, Freud participated in a discourse in regard to civilization which had begun long before the term's appearance in the later eighteenth century. Freud transformed that discourse at a time when, as a result of World War I, the very notion of civilization, one of the hegemonic values of the nineteenth century, had fallen into grave disrepute. In so doing, as in his more strictly psychoanalytic work, he had to take into consideration those whom the nineteenth century had relegated to the margins of or cast beyond the pale of civilization, most notably savages of either the past or present, the lower classes, and women. Sexuality, of course, entered the matter. But however daring and influential Freud's theories in that regard, his major contribution to the discourse concerning civilization resided in his insistence on a matter which had been occasionally raised, only to be immediately buried, in the nineteenth century: the existence within even the most civilized of distinctly savage elements. Like Thomas Hobbes, Freud believed that "*Homo homini lupus.*"[1]

Freud initially eschewed such a sweeping view. The young medical man, very much the product of his class, thought at first in social terms. Visiting Paris in 1885 to work with the great Jean Martin Charcot, he reflected: "The people seem to me of a different species from ourselves. I feel they are all possessed of a thousand demons; instead of 'Monsieur' and 'Voilà l'Echo de Paris' I hear them yelling 'A la lanterne' and 'A bas' this man or that. I don't think they know the meaning of shame or fear....They are a people given to psychical epidemics, historical mass convulsion."[2] While this might have been nothing more than the reaction of a young Viennese bourgeois to the revolutionary capital of Europe, he had already made up his mind about the lower orders: "'the people' judge, think, love and work in a manner utterly different from ourselves."[3] Watching a performance of *Carmen*, it occurred to him that:

> ...the mob gives vent to its appetites, and we deprive ourselves in order to maintain our integrity, we economize in our health, our capacity for enjoyment, our emotions; we save ourselves for something, not knowing for what. And this habit of constant suppression of natural instincts gives us the quality of refine-

ment. We also feel more deeply and so dare not demand much of ourselves. Why don't we get drunk? Because the discomfort and disgrace of the after-effects gives us more 'unpleasure' than the pleasure we derive from getting drunk. Why don't we fall in love with a different person every month? Because at each separation a part of our heart would be torn away. Why don't we make a friend of everyone? Because the loss of him or any misfortune befalling him would affect us deeply. Thus we strive more toward avoiding pain than seeking pleasure.[4]

While the "constant suppression of the natural instincts" would continue to preoccupy him, it is also possible to see here an identification of the people with his later notions of the id and the pleasure principle and that of good bourgeois like Freud and his fiancée with the later ego and the reality principle. However that may be, Freud at this point extended his sympathy to those who lacked his degree of "refinement":

The poor people, the masses could not survive without their thick skins and their easy going ways. Why should they take their relationships seriously when all the misfortunes nature and society have in store for them threatens those they love? The poor are too helpless, too exposed to behave like us. When I see people indulging themselves, disregarding all sense of moderation, I invariably think that this is their compensation for being a helpless target of all the taxes, epidemics, sicknesses, and evils of social institutions.[5]

If this balancing of pleasure and pain revealed a utilitarian bias, that is not surprising, for Freud revered John Stuart Mill, "very possibly…the man of the century most capable of freeing himself of the domination of the usual prejudices."[6]

He found the only fault with his hero to reside in his view of women. Believing Mill's "analogy for the oppression of women in that of the Negro" to be especially absurd, he declared to his fiancée: "Any girl, even without a vote and legal rights, whose hand is kissed by a man willing to risk his all for her love, could have put him right."[7] Hardly prepared for the advent of the "New Woman," he maintained that "all reforming activity, legislation and education, will founder on the fact that long before the age at which a profession can be established in our society, nature will have appointed woman, by her beauty, charm, and goodness, to do something else."[8] Reformers might propose, but Nature disposed. Gesturing vaguely in a progressive direction, he acknowledged a fundamental conservatism: "I adhere to the old ways…legislation and custom have to grant to women many rights kept from them, but the position of women cannot be other than what it is: to be an adored sweetheart in youth, and a beloved wife in maturity."[9] Hardly unusual for his class and generation, such attitudes would be carried into a psychiatric practice concerned largely with women.

Although the friendship eventually ended in bitter recriminations, Freud's early therapeutic and theoretical triumphs and defeats were conveyed, with excitement and agitation, to Wilhelm Fliess, a Berlin nasal specialist at least as imaginative as himself. Gender and class issues inevitably entered the prolonged correspondence. Society, if not yet civilization, also made its appearance. Although surely aware that the American coiner of the neologism "neurasthenia" had linked it closely to civilization, Freud in 1893 insisted upon its sexual origins. As an enlightened physician, he proposed in private correspondence an alternative: "free sexual intercourse between young men and unattached young women."[10] Recognizing that that solution called for "innocuous methods of preventing conception" but suspicious of the condom, he believed that the current situation would continue and perhaps worsen: "masturbation, neurasthenia in the male, hysteroneurasthenia in the female, or syphilis in the male, syphilis in the next generation, gonorrhea in the male, gonorrhea and sterility in the female."[11] With "the lower strata" likely to follow their superiors along this disease-ridden route, "society appears doomed to fall victim to incurable neuroses, which reduce the enjoyment of life to a minimum, destroy marital relations, and bring hereditary ruin to the whole coming generation."[12] Here Freud struck a note characteristic of much of his later work: enlightened prescription and a grim sense of the forces which opposed the implementation of the prescription.

A focus on preordained victimization also appeared. If in Freud's musings to Fliess, woman often appeared as the victim of male inadequacy and privilege, she was also very much the predestined victim. Both frigidity and hysteria sprang from the passivity of the female nature. While Freud's emphasis upon female passivity would be mitigated by his acceptance of Fliess' notion of human bisexuality, he himself contributed to the victimization of women through his stress upon the need for them to make a transition from the sexuality of the clitoris to the vagina. While gender differences remained of paramount importance in explaining different forms of mental malady, class differences also entered the matter. Thus, the lower classes, more immoral and sexually freer than their social superiors, were still open to paranoia, a malady unrelated to either morals or sexuality. The lower classes, at least the servants among them, also posed problems of another order:

> An immense load of guilt, with self-reproaches (for theft, abortion), is made possible by identification

with these people of low morals who are so often remembered, in a sexual connection with father or brother, as worthless female material....Fear of prostitution (fear of being in the street alone), fear of a man hidden under the bed, and so on, also point in the direction of the servant girl. There is a tragic justice in the circumstance that the family head's stooping to a maidservant is atoned for by his daughter's self-abasement.[13]

If the father's behaviour had provoked the hysterical fantasies of his daughter, it was much less clear where the primary responsibility for the seduction resided.

Seduction was of even greater importance in another respect. Freud began by believing his patients' tales of childhood seductions, most frequently by the father. But on September 21, 1897 he announced a change of mind to Fliess.[14] Fantasy, not reality, now lay behind his patients' stories. Although Freud never abandoned a concern with the external world in which children were sexually abused, he now privileged the inner world of psychic dynamics. This transition, like the purportedly necessary transition form the clitoris to the vagina, would have enormous consequences for women.

While corresponding with Fliess, Freud had been hard at work on his first major publications. In 1893, along with Dr. Joseph Breuer, he published "On the Psychical Mechanism of Hysterical Phenomena: Preliminary Communication" in which they stressed the importance of reminiscence in accounting for hysteria. By the time the fuller *Studies in Hysteria* appeared in 1895, sexual problems had assumed pride of place in their explanations. They were careful to note: "Our experience is derived from private practice in an educated and literate social class."[15] Breuer supplied only the case history of the famous "Anna O.," and Freud provided four more such histories. One of them, curiously enough, came from outside the ranks of the "educated and literate social class." It had to do with "Katherina," a servant girl whom Freud had encountered at a rural inn. She had been sexually abused by her father whom Freud, in his first account, changed into her uncle.[16] Whatever the reasons for the change in relationship, Freud claimed to have got to the heart of the matter in a single conversation: "I owed her a debt of gratitude for having made it so much easier for me to talk to her than the prudish ladies of my city practice who regard whatever is natural as shameful."[17] In this case the freer manners of the lower classes had their utility.

In another division of labour, Breuer handled the theoretical section and Freud, the therapeutic, though given the nature of the subject matter, it proved impossible to adhere to so neat a division. In any event, the distinctly Freudian note was there in regard to therapy: "much will be gained in transforming...hysterical misery into common unhappiness."[18] Freud also insisted: "In so far as one can speak of determining causes which lead to the *acquisition* of neuroses, their aetiology is to be looked for in sexual factors."[19] If Breuer eventually grew uneasy with the importance attached to sexuality, even Freud allowed that "the aetiology of the neurosis...is as a rule overdetermined."[20] This degree of subtlety helped him to break with older interpretations:

> We must...keep free from the theoretical prejudice that we are dealing with the abnormal brains of 'dégénérés' and 'déséquilibrés' who are at liberty, owing to a stigmata, to throw overboard the common psychological laws that govern the connection of ideas and in whom any chance idea may become exaggeratedly intense for no motive and another remain

> indestructible for no psychological reason. Experience
> shows that the contrary is true in hysteria.[21]

Here Freud dismissed the conventional wisdom of the previous generation of psychiatrists to which so many of his fel-
low-professionals still cluhg.

Radical as that move was, he believed himself to be far
more radical in his next book, *The Interpretation of Dreams*
(1899). Notable for his articulation of many ideas integral to
his later theory, including the still unnamed Oedipal complex,
he now broke decisively with received wisdom in regard to
normality and abnormality. Citing Schopenhauer who had
called "dreams a brief madness and madness a long dream,"
Freud argued that, while not everybody was insane or even
neurotic, everybody did dream.[22] Dreams, consequently, possessed a universal human significance, and allowed Freud to
maintain that "psychoanalytic research finds no fundamental, but only quantitative distinctions between normal and
neurotic life."[23] Whatever the importance of these quantitative distinctions, Freud here dismissed the nineteenth
century's obsession with drawing firm lines between different conditions, psychic and otherwise. But while introducing ambiguity as the primary intellectual feature of the
twentieth century, this self-perceived scientist could not do
without distinctions of his own.

Often enough they were built upon analogy and
metaphor.[24] His problem was real enough: internal processes
could only be described in terms of the external world. But the
features of that world which Freud drew upon were in themselves revealing. Thus, in discussing the formation of dreams,
he drew upon the relations of entrepreneurs and capitalists.
Moreover, in an image which came more readily to an Austrian
than to an Englishman or an American, he introduced the notion of an internal censor. Very much the product of an age of

imperialism, conquest on the frontiers of knowledge remained very much a part of his self-imagery.

The internal and external worlds were more directly related in *The Psychopathology of Everyday Life* (1901) where he acknowledged, in a footnote, that women possessed a "subtler understanding of unconscious processes."[25] Turning to the acquisition of money and property, he related it to "the primitive greed of the suckling...only...incompletely overcome by civilization and upbringing."[26] Civilization and upbringing as restraining forces also intruded into the servant problem:

> When servants drop fragile articles and so destroy them, our first thought is not of psychological explanation, yet it is not unlikely that here too, obscure motives play their part. Nothing is more foreign to uneducated people than an appreciation of art and works of art. Our servants are dominated by a mute hostility towards the manifestations of art, especially when the objects (whose value they do not understand) become a source of work for them.[27]

Freud, in brief, had his own version of "the servant problem."

Freud later described *The Psychopathology of Everyday Life* as directed towards a popular audience, and much the same could have been said about *Jokes and Their Relationship to the Unconscious* (1905), at least in comparison with other works of the same year. It made clear, however, the way in which his system was based upon psychic economies and expenditures. Again analogy came into play: "I may perhaps venture on a comparison between psychical economy and a business enterprise."[28] But stripped of analogy, the psyche remained strikingly utilitarian: "Dreams serve predominantly for the avoidance of unpleasure, jokes for the attainment of pleasure; but all our mental activities converge in these two aims."[29]

Gender, class and even civilization itself entered into the pleasure derived from humour: "Among country people or in inns of the humbler sort it will be noticed that it is not until the entrance of the barmaid or the innkeeper's wife that smuttiness starts up. Only at higher social levels is the opposite found and the presence of a woman brings smut to an end."[30] Common human drives may have remained the same, but differences in social and cultural development made for differences in their expression:

> It is our belief that civilization and higher education have a large influence in the development of repression....The repressive activity of civilization brings it about that primary possibilities of enjoyment, which have now...been repudiated by the censorship in us, are lost to us. But to the human psyche all renunciation is exceedingly difficult, and so we find that tendentious jokes provide a means of undoing our renunciation and retrieving what we have lost. When we laugh at a refined obscene joke, we are laughing at the same thing that makes a peasant laugh at a coarse piece of smut.[31]

Viewed more generally, civilization and sexuality collided: "There is no more personal claim than that for sexual freedom and at no point has civilization tried to exercise severer repression than in the sphere of sexuality."[32] Yet civilization possessed its advantages for a man of Freud's predilections: "A restriction of our muscular work and an increase of our intellectual work fit in with the course of our personal development towards a higher level of civilization."[33]

With the first devoted to sexual deviancy, the second, to infantile sexuality and the third to puberty, Freud also published his *Three Essays on Sexuality* in 1905. Welcoming the change from a "pathological" to an "anthropological" approach to deviancy, he noted: "It is remarkably widespread among many savage and primitive races, whereas the concept of degeneracy is usually restricted to states of higher civilization (cf. Bloch); and even amongst the civilized peoples of Europe, climate and race exercise the most powerful influence on the prevalence of inversion and upon the attitude towards it."[34] While the invocations of degeneracy and climate were unusual for Freud, his discovery of widespread deviancy among primitives allowed him to link it with the "polymorphous perversity" of the infants of his own world. Human bisexuality lay at the root of these practices. Reduced to its simplest form, the theory had been articulated "by a spokesman of the male inverts: 'a feminine brain in a masculine body.'"[35] Although Freud immediately added that "we are ignorant of what characterizes a feminine brain," ignorance in regard to physiological differences did not prevent him from pronouncing upon other differences: activity characterized the male, passivity, the female.[36] Freud, however, was not simply repeating a truism from the nineteenth century, for the notion of bisexuality allowed for the recognition of these qualities in all humans.

Women still posed a variety of problems. Thus, in his opinion:

> The significance of sexual overvaluation can best be studied in men, for their erotic life alone has been accessible to research. That of women—partly owing to the stunting effect of civilized conditions and partly owing to their conventional secretiveness and insincerity—is still veiled in an impenetrable obscurity.[37]

That argument did not prevent him from continuing to insist on the need for women, at puberty, to change the focus of their sexuality from the clitoris to the vagina. He emphasized the difficulties and dangers involved in that transition:

> The fact that women change their leading erotogenic zone in this way, together with the wave of repression at puberty...are the chief determinants of the greater proneness of women to neurosis and especially to hysteria. The determinants, therefore, are intimately related to the essence of femininity."[38]

If a disposition towards it did not in itself constitute mental malady, Freud readily accepted a greater incidence of mental disturbance among women.

Freud directly confronted the issue in "'Civilized' Sexual Morality and Modern Nervous Illness" (1908).[40] The quotation marks around "Civilized" indicated his unease with a concept more often invoked than realized and, when realized, likely to produce mental sufferings of various degree. Freud began with scholarly references. He cited the Prague philosopher, Christian von Ehrenfel's recent *Sexual Ethics* where he found a distinction between natural and civilized sexual morality, with much criticism of the latter, largely on eugenic grounds. Turning to his own field, he drew upon W. Erb, O. I. Binswanger and the great R. von Krafft-Ebing, all of whom had linked an increase in mental malady to civilization. Freud found their arguments "not...mistaken but insufficient."[41] His own explanation reflected his primary concern: "The injurious influence of civilization reduces itself in the main to the harmful suppression of the sexual life of civilized people (or classes) through the 'civilized' sexual morality prevalent in them."[42] Freud introduced his own version of social contract theory: "Our civilization is built on the suppression of the instincts. Each individual has surrendered some part of his assets....From these contributions has grown civilization's assets in material and ideal life."[43] But even though "sublimation" placed "extraordinarily large amounts of force at the disposal of civilized activity," the strength and constancy of human sexuality still presented civilization with a formidable challenge, the matter being further complicated by the extent to which sexuality and the capacity for its sublimation differed from individual to individual.[44]

Freud posited three stages in the development of civilization: "A first one, in which the sexual instinct may be freely exercised without regard to the aim of reproduction; a second, in which all of the sexual instinct is suppressed except what serves the aims of reproduction; and a third, in which only *legitimate* reproduction is allowed as a sexual aim."[45] Finding the third stage in contemporary conditions, he still took the second stage as the more usual. Even at that stage those unable to conform to civilization's curbing of their sexual drive became either deviants or neurotics. Having dealt with the former group at length in the *Three Essays*, he now devoted closer attention to the neurotics. Excessively moral, these people tried to meet and overfulfill the requirements of civilization:

> For most people there is a limit beyond which their constitution cannot comply with the demands of civilization. All who wish to be more noble-minded than their constitution allows fall victims to neurosis; they would have been more healthy if it could have been possible for them to be less good.[46]

If such was the case with the second stage, Freud found it

> ...easy to predict the result that will follow if sexual freedom is still further circumscribed and the requirements of civilization are raised to the level of the third

stage, which bans all sexual activity outside legal marriage. The number of strong natures who openly oppose the demands of civilization will increase enormously, and so will the number of weaker ones who, faced with the conflict between the pressure of cultural influences and the resistance of their constitution, will take flight into neurotic illness.[47]

That great bourgeois ideal, monogamous marriage, lay at the root of the difficulty.

The sexual ignorance in which bourgeois girls were brought up had nefarious consequences for both partners. But even in the best of circumstances "satisfying sexual intercourse in marriage takes place only for a few years."[48] If women might find another kind of satisfaction in motherhood, Freud noted dryly that infants had a tendency to grow up. Another way out of sexual unhappiness was denied to women, for he believed them to be "only endowed in a small measure with the gift of sublimating their instincts."[49] Largely incapable of contributing to civilization through sublimation, women constituted the principal victims of civilized marriage. There was, of course, an obvious solution: marital infidelity. But if husbands took advantage of the double standard,

...the more strictly a woman has been brought up and the more sternly she has submitted to the demands of civilization the more she is afraid of taking this way out; and in the conflict between her desires and her sense of duty, she once more seeks refuge in a neurosis. Nothing protects her virtue as securely as illness.[50]

If civilization spawned psychic suffering, he was still prepared to consider the proposition that its benefits outweighed its psychic costs.

While Freud admitted an inability "to balance gain against loss correctly," he also announced that he "could advance a great many more considerations on the side of loss."[51] The kind of civilization with which he was familiar worked against itself:

> Neuroses...always succeed in frustrating the purposes of civilization, and in that way actually perform the work of the suppressed mental forces that are hostile to civilization. Thus when society pays for obedience to its far-reaching regulations by an increase in nervous illness, it cannot claim to have purchased a gain at the price of sacrifices; it cannot claim a gain at all.[52]

Well aware of the differences among individuals, Freud refused to provide any general prescriptions. The entire essay, however, implied a call for a loosening of at least some of the restraints imposed upon sexuality by civilization. At this point the enlightened physician was a liberator.

Certainly Freud seemed to be such to some Americans after he delivered in 1909, at the invitation of G. Stanley Hall, the "Five Lectures on Psycho-Analysis." He argued in a once Puritan New England that humans, "with the high standard of our civilization and under the pressure of our internal repression," sought to escape from unsatisfying reality into fantasy.[53] Three routes of escape suggested themselves. First, if sufficiently energetic, one could turn wishes into reality. Second, one might also turn fantasy into art. Third, one could retreat to infantile fantasy and, hence, into neurosis. With success in the world and artistic creativity denied to most people, they stood exposed, depending upon their degree of civilization, to that third possibility. Freud urged that, to avoid it, "we ought not to exalt ourselves so high as completely to neglect what was originally animal in our nature."[54] He added immediately: "Nor should we forget that the satisfaction of the individual's happiness cannot be erased from among the aims of civilization."[55]

Civilization now appeared to show a Janus-face: If the repressions intrinsic to it produced psychic suffering, it also aimed at securing the happiness of the individual. Consequently, "what we call a normal man" was both "the bearer and in part the victim, of the civilization that has been so painfully acquired."[56] Important as individual differences may have been to the practice of psychoanalysis, once Freud introduced the idea of the "normal man," he might have done more in the way of balancing the gains and losses entailed by civilization. The matter was further complicated by his use of quotation marks in regard to the adjective "civilized." Thus, the Americans might be forgiven for seeing him as a liberating opponent of repression when he castigated doctors "under the spell of the combination of prudery and prurience which governs the attitude of most 'civilized' people on matters of sexuality."[57] They were not wholly mistaken, for the quotation marks often indicated not only his suspicion of repression, but also his very real hatred of hypocrisy. Yet, as his reactions to the Americans indicated, Freud remained a supremely civilized Central European gentleman, not altogether at ease with primitives.

Freud was accompanied on his American trip by Carl Jung, the Swiss psychiatrist whom he was grooming to be his successor in the realm of theory. Although their friendship was destined to go the way of the one with Fliess, it too produced a correspondence, whose interest resides less in new theoretical insights on Freud's part than in the stuff of casual exchange. They agreed, for instance, on the relationship between therapy and social class. Working at a public institution, Jung complained of having to deal with uneducated patients. Freud, who had little experience along that line, proved properly sympathetic:

> What with their habits and mode of life, reality is too close to those women to allow them to believe in fantasies. If I had based my theories on the statements of servant girls, they would all be negative. And such behaviour fits in with other peculiarities of that class; well-informed persons assure me that these girls are much less diffident about engaging in coitus than about being seen naked. Fortunately for our therapy, we have previously learned so much from other cases that we can tell these persons their story without having to wait for their contributions. They are willing to confirm what we tell them, but one can learn nothing from them.[58]

If Freud still assumed that their freer sexuality made the lower classes less prone to neurosis, he was prepared to impose upon those who did so suffer the theories which had been derived from his bourgeois patients. The master-listener, in this instance, believed he had nothing to learn from listening.

Contact with Jung stimulated Freud's interest in the possibility of applying psychoanalytic ideas to cultural anthropology, an interest which resulted in *Totem and Taboo* (1912-1913). While his reading ranged from Wilhelm Wundt's *Volkerpsychologie* to Emile Durkheim's recent *Les formes élementaires de la vie religieuse: Le système totemique en Australie* (1912), Freud was most at ease with the English evolutionary anthropologists of the previous generation, people like Lubbock and Tylor whom Darwin had also appreciated. Among his contemporaries, he drew especially on J. G. Frazer's *Totemism and Exogamy* (1912). Like the Englishmen, he sought to work back from the present to the past. He knew that "there have been profound changes in every direction among primitive races, so that it is never possible to decide without hesitation how far their present-day conditions and opinions preserve the primeval past in a petrified form and how far they are modifications."[59] That recognition did not, however, deter the play of his imagination. Largely on the basis of that imagination rather than his reading, Freud unearthed in the prehistoric past a small human horde dominated by a powerful male who monopolized the females; his murder by the resentful younger males who banded together for that purpose; and their consequent feelings which gave rise to totems and taboos which persisted into later religions. Civilization began with this primal parricide. Freud would later describe this bloody version of social contract theory as something "made up on a rainy Sunday afternoon."[60] More seriously, he would also describe it as "a hypothesis, like so many others with which archeologists endeavour to lighten the darkness of prehistoric times—a 'Just So Story' as it was amusingly called by a not unkind English critic."[61]

The book's subtitle clearly stated Freud's primary concern: *Some Points of Agreement between the Mental Lives of Savages and Neurotics.* As he viewed the matter, the parallels between primitives and obsessional neurotics were especially close, with both being torn by a "continuing conflict between the prohibition and the instinct."[62] He had no difficulty in detecting other similarities: primitives and neurotics, for instance, "attach a high valuation—in our eyes an *over*-valuation—to psychic acts."[63] Civilization had retained that emphasis in only one area, that of art. For Freud, the artist resembled the primitive magician or, in views developed elsewhere, the child. Moreover, if the primitive could be compared to the neurotic, he could also be compared to the child. In a very real sense, children, like primitives, inhabited a magical world. The supremely adult Freud had a certain amount of esteem for both, just as he did for the artist, but he no more urged a return to primitivism than he approved flight into neurosis. He preferred to posit a revised Comtean scheme of development: "The human race...have (sic) in the course of the ages developed...three great pictures of the universe: animistic (or mythological), religious and scientific."[64] If most people had not reached the third stage, Freud himself took immense pride in his hard-headed devotion to science.

Freud asserted forcefully his claims for the scientific status of his totalizing intellectual construct in the *Introductory Lectures on Psychoanalysis* (1917):

> What characterizes psychoanalysis as a science is not the material which it handles but the technique with which it works. It can be applied to the history of civilization, to the science of religion and to mythology, not less than to the theory of the neuroses, without doing violence to its essential nature. What it aims at and achieves is nothing other than the unconscious in mental life.[65]

Although Freud was to be accused of spurning the external in favour of the internal world with his abandonment of the seduction theory, he emphasized the interaction between the two spheres. He certainly did not sentimentalize the requirements of social life:

> The motive of human society is in the last resort an economic one; since it does not possess enough provisions to keep its members alive unless they work, it must restrict the number of its members and divert their energies from sexual activity to work. It is faced, in short, by the eternal exigencies of life, which are with us to this day.[66]

Yet whatever the strength of economic necessity, the situation remained precarious: "The sexual instincts are imperfectly tamed and, in the case of every individual who is supposed to join in the work of civilization, there is a risk that his sexual instincts may refuse to be put to that use."[67] As a result of that situation,

> Society believes that no greater threat to its civilization could arise than if the sexual instincts were to be liberated and returned to their original aims. For this reason society does not wish to be reminded of this precarious portion of its foundation….Thus society makes what is disagreeable into what is untrue. It disputes the truth of psychoanalysis with logical and factual arguments; but these arise from emotional sources.[68]

The trick was neat: the opposition between civilization and sexuality was transformed into one between civilization and psychoanalysis which sought to study that sexuality and its multiple ramifications.

Having dismissed logic and facts, the sources of which were tainted, Freud clung to his scientific claims while proffering advice:

> We are not reformers, but merely critical observers; nevertheless, we cannot help observing with a critical eye and we have found it impossible to side with conventional sexual morality or to form a very high opinion of the manner in which society attempts the practical regulation of sexual life. We can present society with a blunt calculation that what is described as morality calls for a bigger sacrifice than it is worth and that its proceedings are not based on honesty and do not display wisdom.[69]

Freud again appeared to favour a relaxation of the sexual constraints imposed by civilization, but he also recognized the
weight of the economic requirements of life. Perhaps that explains his marked reluctance, even at his most liberating, to
provide any indication of how far relaxation should go. He
remained ambivalent about the matter.

No comparable ambivalence can be detected in the distinction he drew, along class lines, between the landlord's
daughter and the caretaker's daughter, both of whom encountered sexuality as children:

> The difference between the lives of these two, in spite
> of their having had the same experience, rests on the
> fact that the ego of one of them underwent a develop-
> ment with which the other never met. Sexual activity
> seemed to the caretaker's daughter just as natural and
> harmless in later life as it had in childhood. The
> landlord's daughter came under the influence of
> education and accepted its demands....Owing to this
> higher moral and intellectual development of her ego
> she came into conflict with the demands of her
> sexuality.[70]

Civilization did its work, and neurosis resulted.

World War I intruded on occasion into these lectures, but
perhaps less than might be expected. With sons serving at the
front and himself exposed to the deprivations of war-time
Vienna, Freud was acutely enough aware of it. Indeed, after a
first flush of Hapsburg loyalty, he wrote to Lou Andreas-
Salomé on November 25, 1914:

> I do not doubt that mankind will survive even this
> war, but I know for me and my contemporaries the
> world will never again be a happy place. It is too

hideous. And the saddest thing about it is that it is exactly the way we should have expected people to behave from our knowledge of psychoanalysis. Because of this attitude to mankind I have never been able to share your blithe optimism. My secret conclusion has always been: since we can only regard the highest present civilization as burdened with an enormous hypocrisy, it follows that we are organically unfitted for it. We have to abdicate, and the Great Unknown, He or It, lurking behind Fate will someday repeat this experiment with another race.[71]

He both developed and modified this grim perspective in the "Thoughts for the Times on War and Death" of 1915.

Again the prospect was bleak enough: "We cannot but feel that no event has ever destroyed so much that is precious in the common possessions of humanity, confused so many of its clearest intelligences, or so thoroughly debased what is highest. Science herself has lost her passionless impartiality."[72] Although writing the latter sentence must have wrung his heart, he found what solace he could in the notion that other times might have been equally hard. Despite this qualification, he admitted that progress itself had been called into question with disillusionment resulting from "the low morality shown externally by states in which in their internal relations pose as guardians of moral standards, and the brutality shown by individuals whom, as participants in the highest human civilization, one would not have thought capable of such behaviour."[73]

Civilization, once again, bore the burden of Freud's accusation:

Our contemporary civilization favours the production...of hypocrisy to an extraordinary degree....Thus there are very many more cultural hypocrites than truly civilized men—indeed it is a debatable point whether a certain degree of cultural hypocrisy is not indispensable for the maintenance of civilization.[74]

Had he elaborated upon the distinction between "cultural hypocrites" and "truly civilized men," Freud might have clarified the ambiguities which stalked his treatments of civilization. But he was more intent upon making the argument that instincts perverted by hypocritical civilization had led to a return to primitivism, a "regression" which was all the easier to accomplish in that "the primitive mind is, in the fullest meaning of the word, imperishable."[75] Having become increasingly convinced of parallels between individual and collective psychologies, Freud found something comparable in the case of nations: "Their interests serve them, at most, as *rationalizations* for their passions; they put forward their interests in order to be able to give reasons for satisfying their passions."[76]

Continuing to pursue the unconscious residue of the primitive in all, Freud turned to death, the primitive view of which he had discussed in *Totem and Taboo*. The war had stripped away "the later accretions of civilization" and revealed "the primal man in each of us."[77] While he deplored the form which this regression had taken, he did not despair of the re-casting of the view of death. Indeed, he welcomed a loosening of the bonds of civilization in this regard:

> Should we not confess that in our civilized attitude towards death we are once again living psychologically beyond our means....Would it not be better to give death the place in reality and in our thoughts which is its due, and to give a little more prominence to the unconscious attitude towards death which we have hitherto so carefully suppressed?[78]

While he recognized that such a move would seem to be "a backward step—a regression," he argued it would "make life more tolerable...once again" and "to tolerate life remains, after all, the first duty of human beings."[79] But Freud refused to indicate just where, on the spectrum between civilized and primitive attitudes and actions, a re-cast position in regard to death should be located. Of course, given the constitutional differences among them, that position would vary from individual to individual, but in this case Freud was also prescribing, in general terms, for social aggregations. Whatever his caution or confusion in this regard, the war had forced a consideration of attitudes toward death.

World War I also drove Freud in theory "beyond the pleasure principle," the title of a work he published in 1920. He had not wholly discounted aggression earlier, but he had always tied it to a more fundamental sexuality. Now he drew a firm distinction between ego instincts, oriented towards death, and the sexual instincts, aiming at life. Going beyond his earlier division of the instincts into "'hunger' and 'love,'" he now subordinated both to a larger *Eros* which sought "to force together and hold together the portions of living substance."[80] *Eros* contended with *Thanatos*, a death instinct which aimed at the restoration of the condition before life. Although the eventual outcome for the individual was clear, the struggle continued throughout life. While reverberations of the war rumbled throughout these arguments, Freud did not introduce the war into them. But they did allow him to formulate an attack upon the ideological construct most damaged by the war, the idea of progress. Integral to many secular notions of civilization, that idea had not hitherto attracted Freud's attention. But he himself had invoked developmental schemes. Even then, however, his psychoanalytic concerns lay with the past and, to a more limited extent, with the present. Aside from his positivist conviction of the advance of science, the future did not especially interest him.

Nor did it much interest fellow-members of the Viennese bourgeoisie of his generation. At the risk of following Freud into the speculatively imaginative realm, it might be suggested that a political "sub-text" lies behind *Beyond the Pleasure Principle*. For that to be followed through upon, the chaos left in the aftermath of the Great War has to be recalled. In any event, Freud set up a purported human instinct towards perfectibility. Aside from philosophers like Condorcet and Godwin at the end of the eighteenth century, and scattered utopians in the nineteenth century, he would have had difficulty in finding proponents of such an instinct. Members of his own class had settled more usually for the conviction that, though threatened by catastrophes like social revolution, bankruptcies, and the seduction of their daughters or wives, things would get better, but not change substantially. Progress, not perfectibility, let alone an instinct oriented toward perfectibility, was the issue.

Freud, in other words, set up a straw-man. He did so at a time when, in their very different fashion, Wilson and Lenin were trying to reduce human misery. Neither the Presbyterian nor the Marxist, however, believed in a human instinct aimed at perfectibility. Perhaps Freud thought of neither, but he did introduce, consciously or unconsciously, an implicitly political note with a sinister juxtaposition:

> The processes involved in the formation of a neurotic phobia, which is nothing else than an attempt at flight from satisfaction of an instinct, present us with a model of this suppositious 'instinct towards perfection'—an instinct which cannot possibly be attributed to *every* human being. The *dynamic* conditions for its development are, indeed, universally present;

but it is only in rare cases that the *economic* situation appears to favour this phenomenon.[81]

Economic conditions in Vienna in 1920 were notoriously grim, and the apolitical liberal Freud might have been trying to warn the Austro-Marxists about their chances for progressive change.[82]

Although inclined to romanticize their freer sexuality, Freud, a good bourgeois, had always been wary of the amoral masses, the social equivalent of his notion of the psychic id. He turned to them directly, in 1921, in *Massenpsychologie und Ich Analyse* or, as the tamer English has it, *Group Psychology and the Analysis of the Ego*. Here he praised the reactionary Gustave Le Bon's "deservedly famous...*Psychologie des foules*."[83] In his view, Le Bon's portrayal of the mass mind did not reveal "a single feature which a psychoanalyst would find any difficulty in placing or in deriving from its source. Le Bon himself shows us the way by pointing to the similarity with the mental life of primitive peoples and of children."[84] More specifically, that meant:

> In groups the most contradictory ideas can exist side by side and tolerate each other, without any conflict arising from the logical contradiction between them. But this is also the case in the unconscious mental life of individuals, of children and of neurotics, as psychoanalysis has long pointed out.[85]

But Le Bon, no psychoanalyst, did not escape criticism. Not only did he lack the concept of repression, but, while comparing the mental condition of the crowd to that of a hypnotized individual, he had paid insufficient attention to the hypnotist. Unfamiliar with the Frenchman's larger body of work, but every bit as much of an elitist, Freud faulted Le Bon for paying insufficient attention to the leadership factor. Curiously, while stressing this factor, Freud paid little attention to the psychology of the leader himself.

Acknowledging that there were different kinds of groups, Freud devoted particular attention to two institutions, the Church and the army. While important, coercion did not sufficiently explain their cohesion. Leadership was pivotal, and integral to it was the illusion of love. As Freud saw the matter: "the same illusion holds good of there being a head—in the Catholic Church Christ; in an army, its Commander-in-Chief—who loves all the individuals in the group with an equal love. Everything depends upon this illusion."[86] The illusion of love, exercised from above, met libidinal forces generated from below: "Each individual is bound by libidinal ties on the one hand to the leader (Christ, the Commander-in-Chief) and on the other hand to the other member of the group."[87]

All of this did not, however, result in a feast of love:

> A religion, even if it calls itself a religion of love, must be hard and unloving to those who do not belong to it. Fundamentally indeed every religion is…a religion of love for all those whom it embraces, while cruelty and intolerance towards those who do not belong to it are natural to every religion.[88]

The issue was all the more pertinent, for "if another group tie takes the place of the religious one—and the socialistic tie seems to be succeeding in doing so—then there will be the same intolerance to outsiders."[89] Always a good liberal, albeit an apolitical liberal, Freud spurned both Catholicism and socialism.

The drive towards equality, which he detected within groups, offended Freud's pronounced individualism. The demand for equality, however, did not refer to the leader. Returning to his "scientific myth of the primal father," he portrayed the group as "a revival of the primal horde. Just as primitive man survives potentially in every individual, so the primal horde may arise once more out of any random collection."[90] In this perspective, little had changed since prehistory: "The leader of the group is still the dreaded primal father; the group still wishes to be governed by unrestricted force; and it has an extreme passion for obedience; in Le Bon's phrase, it has a thirst for obedience."[91] If Freud cannot be blamed for not having foreseen the appearance of a *Führer* who might, indeed, have actually read his book, there was still a slippage in his argument of 1921: the band of parricides in his earlier "Just-So-Story" was missing. Neither an army, nor a Church, nor even a Social Democratic Party, this collective fiction had been made up of revolutionaries. A self-proclaimed rebel against group opinion from his youth but fully capable of exercising ruthless authority over his own group, Freud remained obsessed with leadership at a time when crowns had just fallen throughout Europe. The spectre of revolution might well account for the obsession.

It might also account for another, a momentary change in Freud's thinking in the essay of 1921. Although willing to consider the idea that "a neurosis has the same disintegrating effect upon a group as being in love," he considered it more likely that:

> Where a powerful impetus has been given to group formation neurosis may diminish and, at all events temporarily, disappear....Even those who do not regret the disappearance of religious illusions from the civilized world of today will admit that so long as they were in force they offered those who were bound by them the most powerful protection against the danger of neurosis.[92]

Although he had by no means abandoned his hostility to religion, there was a distinct hint here that it was no longer civilization, with its repressive power, which spawned neurosis, but rather one of its lately emerging components, secularization, which accounted for its flourishing. But if such were the case, then women, much more influenced by religion at the time, should have been more immune to neurosis, a proposition which Freud's system could not allow. In any event, women scarcely came into his analysis of groups unless one wished to complete the equation of groups, primitives, children and neurotics with the further thought that women constituted a majority of the neurotics.

Women reappeared in his essay of 1925, "Some Psychical Consequences of the Anatomical Distinction Between the Sexes." Confronting aging, Freud began on a tentative note, but as so often with him the tentative soon gave way to the categorical. Now accompanied by his final division of the psyche into id, ego and super-ego, he mobilized older ideas: the Oedipus complex, bisexuality, the active masculine, the passive feminine, the need for women to change the focus of their sexuality from clitoris to vagina, and penis-envy. The last, especially, attracted his attention in this effort to show how anatomical differences had psychic consequences. More generally, he declared:

> I cannot evade the notion (though I hesitate to give it ex-
> pression) that for women the level of what is ethically
> normal is different from what it is in men. Their super-
> ego is never so inexorable, so impersonal, so inde-
> pendent of its emotional origins as we require it to be in
> men. Characteristics which critics of every epoch have
> brought up against women—that they show less sense
> of justice than men, that they are less ready to submit to
> the great exigencies of life, that they are more influenced

in their judgments by feeling of affection or hostility—
all these would be amply accounted for by the modifica-
tion in the formation of their super-ego.[93]

Caution is called for here, for while he repeated truisms of
the ages, Freud was no special friend to the super-ego, that
psychic manifestation of civilization. Moreover, he tried to
offer an olive-branch of a sort to women and their friends:

> We must not allow ourselves to be deflected by the
> denials of the feminists, who are anxious to force us to
> regard the two sexes as completely equal in position
> and worth; but we shall...willingly agree that the
> majority of men are also far behind the masculine idea
> and that all human beings, as a result of their bisexual
> disposition and of cross-inheritance, combine in them-
> selves both masculine and feminine characteristics, so
> that pure masculinity and femininity remain theoreti-
> cal constructions of uncertain content.[94]

Just how "activity" and "passivity" related to this "uncertain
content" remained unclear.

Despite the introduction of a fictional interlocutor whom he
treated courteously, no olive-branch appeared in his next major
endeavour, *The Future of an Illusion* (1927). Religion constituted
the illusion, and, in the best of Freudian worlds, it would have
no future. Having hitherto shown a singular lack of interest in
the future, he underscored the difficulties and dangers of
prophecy. But he was now prepared to speculate about the future of civilization or, more narrowly, its religious component.
He defined civilization in the most general terms as:

> ...all those respects in which human life has raised it-
> self above its animal status....It includes on the one

hand all the knowledge and capacity that men have
acquired in order to control the forces of nature and
extract its wealth for the satisfaction of human needs,
and, on the other hand, all the regulations necessary
in order to adjust the relations of men to one another
and especially the distribution of available wealth.[95]

Put crudely, civilization entailed the exploitation of Nature
and people.

If civilization served human needs and really defined the
human, many people experienced it as a burden for essentially
social reasons: "One...gets the impression that civilization is
something which was imposed on a resisting majority by a
minority who understood how to obtain possession of the
means to power and coercion."[96] Faced with this situation, he
was prepared to consider a utopian solution:

One would think that a re-ordering of human relations should be possible, which would remove the
sources of dissatisfaction by renouncing coercion and
the suppression of the instincts, so that, undisturbed
by internal discord, men might devote themselves to
the acquisition of wealth and its enjoyment.[97]

However attractive that prospect might be, he dismissed it as
unfeasible:

It is just as impossible to do without control of the
mass by a minority as it is to dispense with coercion in
the work of civilization. For masses are lazy and unin-
telligent; they have no love for instinctual renuncia-
tion, and they are not to be convinced by argument of
its inevitability; and the individuals composing them
support one another in giving free reign to their indis-

cipline. It is only through the influence of individuals who can set an example and whom the masses recognize as their leaders, that they can be induced to perform the work and undergo the renunciations on which the existence of civilization depends.[98]

Certainly never a democrat, Freud vigorously maintained that

> ...there are two widespread human characteristics which are responsible for the fact that the regulations of civilization can only be maintained by a certain degree of coercion—namely, that men are not fond of work and that arguments are of no avail against their passions.[99]

With his acceptance of it eased by those "mental assets" which were intended "to reconcile men to it and to recompense them for their sacrifices," Freud now made explicit what had been implicit in even his most liberating discussions of civilization.[100] If he did not spell out the necessary "certain degree of coercion" which it required, he now championed civilization:

> Probably a certain percentage of mankind (owing to a pathological disposition or an excess of instinctual strength) will always remain asocial; but if it were feasible merely to reduce the majority that is hostile to civilization today into a minority, a great deal would have been accomplished.[101]

By now, Freud's lingering affection for heroic rebel had wholly disappeared.

As matters stood, social relations, essentially the class factor, constituted the nub of the problem. While suspicious of the drives and consequent discontents which pertained to all humans, he especially concerned himself with the more specifically discontented:

> If…a culture has not got beyond the point at which the satisfaction of one portion of its participants depends upon the suppression of another, and perhaps larger portion—and this is the case in all present-day culture—it is understandable that the suppressed people should develop an intense hostility toward a culture whose existence they make possible by their work, but in whose wealth they have too little a share.[102]

He then judged harshly: "It goes without saying that a civilization which leaves so large a number of its participants unsatisfied and drives them into revolt neither has nor deserves the prospect of a lasting existence."[103] But he had not become a Bolshevik or even a Social Democrat, for he detected checks upon the drive towards revolt:

> The narcissistic satisfaction provided by the cultural ideal is…among the forces which are successful in combating hostility to culture within the cultural unit. The satisfaction can be shared in not only by the favoured classes, which enjoy the benefit of culture, but also by the suppressed ones, since the right to despise the people outside it compensates them for the wrongs they suffer within their own unit.[104]

Without taking this factor into account, "it would be impossible to understand how a number of civilizations have survived so long in spite of the justifiable hostility of large human masses."[105]

If art provided some people with "substitute satisfactions for the oldest and still most deeply felt cultural renunciations," it was eclipsed in significance by religious ideas, "perhaps the most important item in the psychical inventory of a civilization."[106] The role of religious ideas turned upon civilization's antagonistic relation to nature: "the principal task of civilization, its actual *raison d'être*, is to defend us against nature."[107] However committed Freud had been to a loosening of the bonds of civilization, this defensive role precluded any calls for "the abolition of civilization."[108] Were humans to return to the state of nature through such an abolition, they would be in for a shock:

> It is true that nature would not demand any restrictions of instinct from us, she would let us do as we liked; but she has her own peculiarly effective method or restricting us. She destroys us—coldly, cruelly, relentlessly...and possibly through those very things that occasioned our satisfaction.[109]

Confronted with nature's grim world, humans had created civilization with its initially vital religious component.

If religion was an "illusion," it had utility in the past. Even in the present, religion as "universal neurosis" had a utility of a sort: "devout believers are safeguarded in a high degree against the risk of certain neurotic illnesses."[110] But there was now the possibility of a preferable alternative to religion, the possibility of an *"education to reality."*[111] While he acknowledged that his hopes might prove illusory, Freud was uncharacteristically optimistic: "The voice of the intellect is a soft one, but it does not rest till it has gained a hearing. Finally, after a countless succession of rebuffs, it succeeds....The primacy of the intellect lies...in a distant, distant future, but probably not in an *indefinitely* distant one."[112] The hegemony of science, rather than religion, provided the measure by which the best of all, though still inevitably imperfect, civilizations might be judged and acclaimed. Freud returned to the matter in a grimmer mood in his great essay of 1930, *Civilization and Its Discontents*. He repeated the definition of three years earlier:

> The word 'civilization' describes the whole sum of the achievements and the regulations which distinguish our lives from those of our animal ancestors and which serve two purposes—namely to protect men against nature and to adjust their mutual relations.[113]

Science and technology had served the first purpose so successfully that "man has...become a kind of prosthetic God."[114] Moreover, nodding in the direction of progress, there would surely be more to come. However, recoiling from the notion of progress, Freud noted that, despite such advances, humans had not become happier. While vitally important, science and technology were not the only components of civilization.

There were other human needs. Although it possessed no immediate utilitarian character, humans also hankered after beauty. Cleanliness was also not to be disregarded: the use of soap had actually come to be regarded as "an actual component of civilization."[115] Order, however, was of even greater importance. But Freud subordinated both cleanliness and order to another factor: "No feature...seems better to characterize civilization than the esteem and encouragement of man's higher mental activities—his intellectual, scientific, and artistic achievements—and the leading role that it assigns to ideas in human life."[116] With all of them aiming at "the confluent goals of utility and a yield of pleasure," he brought together the religious ideas treated three years before, the "speculations" of philosophy, and "ideals," by which he meant "ideas of a possible perfection of individuals or of peoples or of the whole of humanity."[117] Freud had remained a utilitarian, but he had done so in his own fashion, and that fashion required a cautionary note: "judgments of value" should not mislead in regard to

> ...any particular religion, or philosophic system, or ideal. Whether we think we find in them the highest achievements of the human spirit, or where we deplore them as aberrations, we cannot but recognize that where they are present, and, especially, where they are dominant, a high level of civilization is implied.[118]

The problem within civilization remained that of social relations, "the relation of men to one another...relationships which affect a person as a neighbour, as a source of help, as another person's sexual object, as a member of a family and of a State."[119] Although the class factor had been dropped—to introduce it, Freud would have had to substitute "source of exploitation" for "source of help"—he remained acutely aware of the social dimension of life:

> Human life in common is only made possible when a majority comes together which is stronger than separate individuals and which remains united against separate individuals. The power of this community is then set up as 'right' in opposition to the power of the individual who is condemned as 'brute force.' This replacement of the power of the individual by the power of the community constitutes the decisive step of civilization.[120]

Consequently, he concluded:

> The first requisite of civilization...is that of justice—
> that is, the assurance the a law once made will not be
> broken in favour of an individual. This implies noth-
> ing as to the ethical value of such a law. The final
> course of cultural development seems to tend towards
> making the law no longer an expression of the will of a
> small community—a caste or a stratum of the popula-
> tion or a racial group—which, in its turn, behaves like
> a violent individual towards other, and perhaps more
> numerous, collections of people. The final outcome
> should be a rule of law to which all—except those who
> are not capable of entering a community—have con-
> tributed by a sacrifice of their instincts, and which
> leaves no one—again with the same exception—at the
> mercy of brute force.[121]

Freud, in other words, accepted that great bourgeois ideal,
equality before the law. His conclusions, implicit and explicit,
are all the more interesting.

Implicitly, like the revolutionaries of 1789, he believed that
those incapable of entering the community—the mad, children,
and women—had no right to participate in the body politic. But
1930 was not 1789. Hence, whatever "the final outcome," he
ridiculed "the prejudice that civilization is synonymous with
perfecting."[112] Moreover, it appeared that justice was every bit
as much an illusion as the religion of which it constituted a vital
component. He was left with the problem which had bedeviled
capitalist society since its development: the relationship between the individual and society. Whatever the differences
among the three thinkers, Freud supplied an interpretation
which Hobbes and Rousseau would have understood:

> The liberty of the individual is no gift of civilization. It
> was greatest before there was any civilization, though

then, it is true, it had for the most part no value, since the individual was scarcely in a position to defend it. The development of civilization imposes restrictions on it, and justice demands that no one shall escape these restrictions.[123]

Social contract theory had assumed a form congruent with the demands of the twentieth century.

Individuals had traded liberty for security, but they resented the terms of the trade. Hence,

...a good part of the struggles of mankind centre round the single task of finding an expedient accommodation—one, that is, that will bring happiness—between the claim of the individual and the cultural claims of the group; and one of the problems that touches the fate of humanity is whether such an accommodation can be reached by means of some particular form of civilization or whether the conflict is irreconcilable.[124]

Groping towards an identity of the interests of individual and society, a similarity in developments struck Freud:

The process of the civilization of the human species is...an abstraction of a higher order than is the development of the individual and it is therefore harder to apprehend in concrete terms; nor should we pursue analogies to an obsessive extreme; but in view of the similarities between the aims of the two processes—in one case the integration of a separate individual into a human group, and in the other case the creation of a unified group out of many individuals—we cannot be surprised at the similarity between the means employed and the resultant phenomena.[125]

According to Freud, the individual had renounced certain forms of pleasure, while continuing to crave them unconsciously, and society had also made its renunciations, most notably in connection with the religious "illusion."

Possessed of an intellectual neatness, this solution posed its own problems. Freud carried the comparison furthest in positing the existence of a civilizational super-ego:

> The super-ego of an epoch of civilization has an origin similar to that of an individual. It is based on the impression left behind by the personalities of great leaders—men of overwhelming force of mind or men in whom one of the human impulses has found its strongest and purest, and therefore often its most one-sided, expression.[126]

If the elitist Freud seldom had difficulties with leadership, the moralistic super-ego, fuelled by the energies of the id, continued to give him trouble. However necessary for the continued existence of humans as humans, both the collective and the individual super-egos remained suspect in his eyes. He registered his ambivalence with an extreme example:

> The commandment, 'Love thy neighbour as thyself,' is the strongest defence against human aggressiveness and an excellent example of the unpsychological proceedings of the cultural super-ego. The commandment is impossible to fulfil; such an enormous inflation of love can only lower its value, not get rid of the difficulty. Civilization pays no attention to all this; it merely admonishes us that the harder it is to obey the

precept the more meritorious it is to do so. But anyone
who follows such a precept in present-day civilization
only puts himself at a disadvantage vis-à-vis the person who disregards it.[127]

As such a morality would not be rewarded, Freud believed the
problem it posed to be insurmountable.

Freud did allow that "a real change in the relations of
human beings to possessions would be of more help in this
direction than any ethical commandments."[128] If socialists had
got that right, they had also confused the matter through an
excessively optimistic view of human nature, something of
which Freud could never be accused. Property, in his view,
constituted less of a problem than labour. He asserted flatly:
"The interest of work in common would not hold civilization
together; individual passions are stronger than reasonable interests."[129] According to Freud the liberal: "The great majority
of people only work under the stress of necessity, and this
natural human aversion to work raises the most difficult social
problems."[130] This sombre view of human nature stood in stark
contrast to that of the communists. While he refused to involve
himself with "any economic criticisms of the communist system," Freud did insist:

> In abolishing private property we deprive the human
> love of aggression of one of its instruments, certainly a
> strong one, though certainly not the strongest; but we
> have in no way altered the differences in power and
> influence which are misused by aggressiveness, nor
> have we altered anything in nature. Aggressiveness
> was not created by property. It reigned almost without
> limit in primitive times, when property was still very
> scanty, and it already shows itself in the nursery al-
> most before property has given up its primal, anal

form; it forms the basis of every relation of affection and love among people (with the single exception, perhaps, of the mother's relation to her male child).[131]

This concern with aggression permitted him to wonder, only a few years before the beginning of the purges, "what the Soviets will do after they have wiped out their bourgeoisie."[132]

Freud had now found aggression at play practically everywhere, even in the realm of sexuality, whose subversive power he never discounted. Indeed, as a consequence of the "primary mutual hostility of human beings, civilized society is perpetually threatened with disintegration."[133] Yet, however constant this grave threat, he thought it "always possible to bind together a considerable number of people in love, so long as there are other people left over to receive the manifestation of their aggressiveness."[134] He observed sardonically: "In this respect the Jewish people, scattered everywhere, have rendered most useful services to the civilizations of the countries that have been their hosts."[135] To drive the point home, he asserted: "When once the Apostle Paul had posited universal love between men as the foundation of the Christian community, extreme intolerance on the part of Christendom towards those outside it became the inevitable consequence."[136] Civilizations, like individuals, did not love their neighbours as themselves.

Civilization curbed and fed upon instincts which had been renounced by individuals in whom their strength remained unimpaired. The situation fostered a sense of guilt: "Inevitably the price we pay for our advance in civilization is a loss of happiness through the heightening of the sense of guilt."[137] Inevitably, the question of the balance sheet of civilization, the question of its benefits and costs, again arose. Certainly, its scientific component defended humans against nature, but now Freud was less sanguine than he had been only three years before: "Men have gained control over the forces of nature to such an extent that with their help they would have no difficulty in exterminating one another to the last man."[138] Science, the fruit of civilization, now threatened to destroy civilization. In that respect Freud had "worked through" the lessons of World War I.

Fully convinced that individuals were swayed by *Thantos*, the death instinct which could only be countered by *Eros*, he found the relationship of the latter to civilization to be ambiguous. Giving rise to the family and friendship, *Eros* contributed initially to the rise and consolidation of civilization. But the relationship between love and civilization gave rise to a multitude of conflicts, not least the Oedipal complex. Society or civilization had worked out the means of dealing with problems like detaching the male youth from his family, but there still remained the fundamental problem of women. If they had supplied the initial impetus to civilization through "the claims of their love," very shortly thereafter they had come "into opposition to civilization" and henceforth exercised a "retarding and restraining influence" in regard to it.[139] They did so as representatives of "the interests of the family and of sexual life."[140] Given the primacy of these female concerns, "the work of civilization" became "increasingly the business of men," confronting them "with ever more difficult tasks" and compelling them "to carry out instinctual sublimations of which women are little capable."[141] Here the economy of energy asserted itself: what the male expended through his participation in civilization, he withdrew from the women and the family. Consequently, "the woman finds herself forced into the background by the claims of civilization and she adopts a hostile attitude towards it."[142]

Attempting to describe the situation, Freud once again brought together social oppression and individual repression through analogy: "civilization behaves towards sexuality as a

people or a stratum of the population does which has sub-
jected another one to its exploitation. Fear of a revolt by the
suppressed elements drives it to strict precautionary
measures."[143] Born into the Jewish bourgeoisie of the Austro-
Hungarian empire, Freud had no more difficulty in dealing
with national and class differences than he had in re-telling
the purportedly revealing story of "the peasant woman who
complained that her husband did not love her any more, since
he had not beaten her for a week."[144] Freud drew upon this
folkloric wisdom, a standard item in the sexological literature
at the turn of the century, to illustrate the link between aggression and sexuality dangerously ignored within the kind of
civilization which had reached a "high-water mark" in contemporary Europe.[145]

Writing at a time when many of the nineteenth-century
shibboleths against which he had initially struggled had dis-
solved, Freud still presented himself as a liberator. But now explicit qualifications accompanied his message. Thus, while he
still argued that the matter had been carried much too far, he
acknowledged: "A cultural community is perfectly justified,
psychologically, in starting by proscribing manifestations of
the sexual life of children, for there would be no prospect of
curbing the sexual lusts of adults if the ground had not been
prepared in childhood."[146] Still nursing something of his old
sympathy for those strong enough to defy the proscriptions of
a hypocritical civilization, Freud disavowed any intention of
expression of an opinion on the value of civilization. If he was
coyly disingenuous in the disavowal, he was more honest in
refusing to be a "prophet" who offered "consolation."[147] His
hopes, at best, were modest:

> We may expect gradually to carry through such an al-
> teration to civilization as will better satisfy our needs
> and will escape criticism. But perhaps we may also

> familiarize ourselves with the idea that there are dif-
> ficulties attaching to the nature of civilization which
> will not yield to any attempt at reform.[148]

Having bowed slightly in the direction of progress, he still presented civilization as a trade-off between security and personal happiness. With the hopes of older generations of liberals disappointed, the apolitical liberal Freud had tried to loosen, to an unspecified degree, the constraints of civilization, but this also involved a lowering of expectations regarding what civilization did and could provide. Committed to psychic book-keeping, this heir of the utilitarians refused to draw up, in any specific detail, the balance sheets of civilization.

Freud's caution in this regard made sense in the wake of World War I which had severely shaken faith in Enlightenment values, not least the notions of civilization and progress. Yet, in his scientistic positivism and consequent hostility to religion, he remained faithful to the Enlightenment. He also did so in another fashion. Viewed superficially, a considerable distance seems to divide the Enlightenment notion of civilization as the refinement of manners and the Freudian notion of it as primarily a matter of constraint and repression. The Enlightenment, however, did not entirely overlook the latter factors. Writing of West Africans at the end of the eighteenth century, the explorer Mungo Park observed: "the maternal affection (neither suppressed by the restraints nor diverted by the solicitudes of civilized life) is everywhere conspicuous among them."[149]

If in a fashion Freud remained faithful to the Enlightenment, he also remained faithful to his class. While he hated the hypocrisy perhaps intrinsic to a bourgeoisie which prided itself on its degree of civilization, Freud never allowed his distaste to drive him towards primitivism. Seen in terms of his system, such a move would have brought him into all too close a proximity to the lower orders whom he feared. These people, the savages within civilization, constituted the social expression of the id. Indeed, Freud's entire topography of the psyche had a social dimension. Firmly committed to the primacy of the ego, he presented it very much as the good bourgeois, wheeling and dealing in a hostile world and threatened internally by the demands of the id and a super-ego which drew upon the energies of the id. That super-ego, in turn, might have stood for the Catholic Church which in Austria comprised masses mobilized by the anti-Semitic Christian Social movement. Be that as it may, the super-ego embodied the demands of civilization. With those demands fostering hypocrisy, Freud called for a lessening of their intensity. But he did not abandon civilization. It constituted one of the standards by which he judged primitives abroad, savages at home, and women. In doing so, Freud participated in a process of judgement and equation which had begun long before the word "civilization" had appeared, but a process facilitated by its appearance.

However the word was defined, during the nineteenth century it became all too easy to relegate a variety of groups to the margins of civilization or to cast them beyond its borders. Non-European peoples, the labouring classes, criminals, the mad and women, frequently equated with each other, all suffered this fate. The outbreak and murderous prolongation of World War I, however, brought the very idea of civilization into question. If it were to survive, it would have to be reformulated in light of the grim conditions of the twentieth century. Freud provided a reformulation which took into account a nightmare which occasionally had come to the surface in the nineteenth century, only to be almost always immediately disavowed. Without abandoning value judgements regarding distinct groups, he acknowledged the savage element within everybody. Resting much more on speculative supposition than science, his judgment seemed to be confirmed by the subsequent course of the century. If Freud himself remained ambivalent about the benefits and costs of civilization, he had recast the problem of the relationship between the individual and society which had dogged capitalism since the seventeenth century when, universalizing like Freud, Thomas Hobbes also proclaimed humans to be wolves unto each other. Hobbes sought a political solution to the problem in the absolute power of the sovereign. With many of the political solutions proffered in his day posing a distinct threat to himself and the values he cherished, Freud found his solution in something more amorphous but equally constraining civilization.

NOTES

1. Sigmund Freud, *Civilization and Its Discontents* (New York: W.W. Norton & Co., 1961), p. 58.
2. Sigmund Freud to Minna Bernays, Dec. 3, 1885, Ernst L. Freud (ed.), *The Letters of Sigmund Freud* (New York: Basic Books, 1975), pp. 187-88.
3. Freud to Martha Bernays, Aug. 29, 1883, *Ibid.*, p. 51.
4. *Ibid.*, p. 50.
5. *Ibid.*, p. 51.
6. Freud to Martha Bernays, Nov. 15, 1883, *Ibid.*, p. 75.
7. *Ibid.*, p. 76.
8. *Ibid.*
9. *Ibid.*
10. "Draft B. The Etiology of the Neuroses," Feb. 3, 1893, Jeffrey M. Masson (ed.), *The Complete Letters of Sigmund Freud to Wilhelm Fliess* (Cambridge: Harvard University Press, 1985), p. 44.
11. *Ibid.*
12. *Ibid.*
13. "Draft L. The Architecture of Hysteria," May 2, 1897, *Ibid.*, p. 241.
14. Jeffrey M. Masson has charged that the change of mind came from Freud's exculpatory reaction to Fliess' botched operation on the nose of one of Freud's patients. For details, see Jeffrey M. Masson, *The Assault on Truth: Freud's Suppression of the Seduction Theory* (New York: Farrar, Straus and Giroux, 1984).
15. Sigmund Freud and Joseph Breuer, *Studies in Hysteria* (Harmondsworth: Penguin Books, 1974), p. 47.

16. Freud corrected himself in the 1924 edition where he explained: "Distortions like the one I introduced in the present instance should be altogether avoided in reporting a case history." *Ibid.*, no. 2, p. 201. He did not explain the reasons for the distortion.
17. *Ibid.*, p. 198.
18. *Ibid.*, p. 393.
19. *Ibid.*, p. 346.
20. *Ibid.*
21. *Ibid.*, p. 380.
22. Sigmund Freud, *The Interpretation of Dreams* (Harmondsworth: Penguin Books, 1976), p. 162.
23. *Ibid.*, p. 497.
24. Claiming scientific status for his work, Freud would later rank his achievement with those of Copernicus and Darwin. Yet in the works of no other scientist does one find extensive Index entries for analogy.
25. Sigmund Freud, *The Psychopathology of Everyday Life* (Harmondsworth: Penguin Books, 1976), fn. 1, p. 208.
26. *Ibid.*, p. 210.
27. *Ibid.*, pp. 227-28.
28. Sigmund Freud, *Jokes and Their Relation to the Unconscious* (Harmondsworth: Penguin Books, 1976) p. 210.
29. *Ibid.*, p. 238.
30. *Ibid.*, p. 143.
31. *Ibid.*, p. 145.
32. *Ibid.*, pp. 155-56.
33. *Ibid.*, p. 255.
34. "Three Essays on Sexuality," Sigmund Freud, *On Sexuality* (Harmondsworth: Penguin Books, 1977) pp. 33-169, p. 49.
35. *Ibid.*, p. 54.
36. *Ibid.*
37. *Ibid.*, p. 63. Freud's startling ignorance in regard to women would be well illustrated by the case history of "Dora," which he also published in 1905. Describing her disgusted reaction to the kiss of "Herr K," Freud maintained: "This was surely the situation to call up a distinct feeling of sexual excitement in a girl of fourteen who had never before been approached." He went on to affirm categorically: "I would without question consider a person hysterical in whom an occasion for sexual excitement elicited feelings that were predominantly or exclusively unpleasurable." Neither age, nor ignorance, nor degree of cultivation, nor even confusion came into the matter. "Dora," Sigmund Freud, *Case Histories*, I, *Dora and Little Hans* (Harmondsworth: Penguin Books, 1977), pp. 31-164, p. 59.
38. Freud, "Three Essays," p. 144.
39. *Ibid.*, p. 168.

40. The German title was "Die 'Kulturelle' Sexualmoral und die Moderne Nervosität." Freud announced in 1927: "I scorn to distinguish between culture and civilization." Freud, *Future of an Illusion*, p. 2.
41. "'Civilized' Sexual Morality and Modern Nervous Illness," Sigmund Freud, *Civilization, Society and Religion* (Harmondsworth: Penguin Books, 1985) pp. 33-55, p. 37.
42. *Ibid.*
43. *Ibid.*, p. 39.
44. *Ibid.*
45. *Ibid.*, p. 41.
46. *Ibid.*, p. 43.
47. *Ibid.*, p. 44.
48. *Ibid.*, p. 46.
49. *Ibid.*
50. *Ibid.*, p. 47.
51. *Ibid.*, pp. 47-48.
52. *Ibid.*, p. 54.
53. Sigmund Freud, *Five Lectures on Psycho-Analysis* (New York: W. W. Norton & Co., 1989) p. 55.
54. *Ibid.*, p. 61.
55. *Ibid.*
56. *Ibid.*, p. 37.
57. *Ibid.*, p. 43.
58. Freud to Carl Jung, Jun 14, 1907, William McGuire (ed.), *The Freud/Jung Letters: The Correspondence between Sigmund Freud and C. G. Jung* (Princeton: Princeton University Press, 1974), p. 65.
59. "Totem and Taboo," Sigmund Freud, *The Origin of Religion* (Harmondsworth: Penguin Books, 1985), fn. 1, p. 161.
60. Quoted in Ronald W. Clark, *Freud: The Man and the Cause* (New York: Random House, 1980), p. 355.
61. Sigmund Freud, *Group Psychology and the Analysis of the Ego* (New York: W.W. Norton & Co., 1959), p. 54.
62. Freud, "Totem and Taboo," p. 83.
63. *Ibid.*, p. 147.
64. *Ibid.*, p. 134.
65. Sigmund Freud, *Introductory Lectures on Psychoanalysis* (Harmondsworth: Penguin Books, 1973), pp. 436-37.
66. *Ibid.*, pp. 353-54
67. *Ibid.*, p. 48.
68. *Ibid.*
69. *Ibid.*, p. 485.
70. *Ibid.*, p. 399.
71. Freud to Lou Andreas, Nov. 25, 1914, Ernst Pfeiffer (ed.), *Sigmund Freud and Lou Andreas Salomé Letters* (New York: W.W. Norton & Co., 1985), p. 21.

72. "Thoughts for the Times on War and Death," Freud, *Civilization*, pp. 57-89, p. 61.
73. *Ibid.*, p. 67.
74. *Ibid.*, p. 72.
75. *Ibid.*, p. 73.
76. *Ibid.*, p. 75.
77. *Ibid.*, p. 88.
78. *Ibid.*, p. 89.
79. *Ibid.*
80. Sigmund Freud, *Beyond the Pleasure Principle* (New York: W.W. Norton & Co., 1961), p. 45, fn. 1, p. 55.
81. *Ibid.*, p. 36.
82. Freud's recalcitrant patient of the first decade of the century, "Dora," had a brother, Otto Bauer, who as one of the leaders of Austrian Social Democracy was trying in 1920 to stake out a position between those of the Second and the Third Internationals.
83. Freud, *Group Psychology*, p. 4.
84. *Ibid.*, p. 9.
85. *Ibid.*, p. 11.
86. *Ibid.*, p. 26. In Freud's view, when measured by this standard, German military leadership during the war had proven remarkably inept.
87. *Ibid.*, p. 27.
88. *Ibid.*, p. 30.
89. *Ibid.*, p. 31.
90. *Ibid.*, p. 55.
91. *Ibid.*, p. 59.
92. *Ibid.*, p. 74.
93. "Some Psychical Consequences of the Anatomical Distinction Between the Sexes," Freud, *On Sexuality*, p. 342.
94. *Ibid.*
95. Freud, *Future of an Illusion*, pp. 2-3.
96. *Ibid.*, p. 4.
97. *Ibid.*, pp. 4-5. He was more cautious in regard to the less utopian Bolshevism: "I have not the least intention of making judgments on the great experiment in civilization that is now in progress in that vast country that stretches between Europe and Asia. I have neither the special knowledge nor the capacity to decide on its practicality, to test the expediency of the methods employed or to measure the width of the inevitable gap between intentions and execution." *Ibid.*, pp. 8-9.
98. *Ibid.*, pp. 5-6.
99. *Ibid.*, p. 6.
100. *Ibid.*, p. 11.
101. *Ibid.*, p. 8.
102 *Ibid.*, p. 15.
103. *Ibid.*, pp. 15-16.

104. *Ibid.*, p. 17.
105. *Ibid.*
106. *Ibid.*, p. 18.
107. *Ibid.*, p. 20.
108. *Ibid.*
109. *Ibid.*
110. *Ibid.*, p. 72.
111. *Ibid.*, p. 81. Freud did not think that religion could be done away with "by force and at a single blow," an undertaking which he likened to the American experiment with Prohibition, itself partially the result of "petticoat government." *Ibid.*, p. 80.
112. *Ibid.*, pp. 87-88.
113. Freud, *Civilization and its Discontents*, p. 36.
114. *Ibid.*, pp. 38-39.
115. *Ibid.*, p. 40.
116. *Ibid.*, p. 41.
117. *Ibid.*
118. *Ibid.*
119. *Ibid.*, p. 42.
120. *Ibid.*
121. *Ibid.*
122. *Ibid.*, p. 43.
123. *Ibid.*, pp. 42-43.
124. *Ibid.*, p. 43.
125. *Ibid.*, p. 87.
126. *Ibid.*, p. 88.
127. *Ibid.*, p. 90.
128. *Ibid.*
129. *Ibid.*, p. 59.
130. *Ibid.*, fn. 1, p. 27.
131. *Ibid.*, p. 60.
132. *Ibid.*, p. 62.
133. *Ibid.*, p. 59.
134. *Ibid.*, p. 61.
135. *Ibid.*
136. *Ibid.*
137. *Ibid.*, p. 81.
138. *Ibid.*, p. 92.
139. *Ibid.*, p. 50.
140. *Ibid.*
141. *Ibid.*
142. *Ibid.*, p. 51.
143. *Ibid.*
144. *Ibid.*, fn. 3, p. 53.
145. *Ibid.*, p. 51.

146. *Ibid.*
147. *Ibid.*, p. 92.
148. *Ibid.*, p. 62.
149. Mungo Park, *Travels in the Interior District of Africa, 1795-97* (London: J.M. Dent & Sons, 1907), p. 202.

CONCLUSION

It IS DIFFICULT not to share Freud's ambivalence regarding civilization, though for different reasons than his own. If judgements of cultural superiority and inferiority had a long history in the West and elsewhere in places like China, the appearance of the term in the late eighteenth century facilitated them. Open to a variety of interpretations, civilization provided a handy shorthand by which to judge aboriginal peoples, the working classes, criminals and lunatics, children and women, who were perceived as residing at the margins or beyond the borders of civilization. Often these groups were equated with each other. Freud was very much a part of this tradition of discourse. Thus, he could argue:

> Among races at a low level of civilization, and among the lower strata of civilized races, the sexuality of children seems to be given free rein. This probably provides a powerful protection against the sub-

sequent development of neuroses in the individual. But does it not at the same time involve an extraordinary loss of aptitude for cultural achievements?[1]

A witness to the age of imperialism, this explorer of the psyche had no hesitation about referring to the sexual life of women as "a 'dark continent.'"[2] Viewed in light of his equations and metaphors, Freud's ideas appear to be much less radical than is sometimes supposed.

Yet, if Freud was but one participant in a long debate concerning civilization, he also changed decisively the terms of that debate. Reacting to the events of the twentieth century by acknowledging the potential for reversion to savagery within all humans, he introduced a greater degree of toleration into the discourse. If the discontented could be found in specific groups, the discontents were universal and likely to be increased by the constraints, the repressions imposed by civilization. Hating the hypocrisy which he suspected might be integral to his own civilization, he called for a loosening of those bonds. But he was never too clear about what such a loosening would entail or how far it should go.

One can but surmise that this cultivated gentleman, who prided himself on the grimness of his philosophy, would be appalled at how far the liberalization of the constraints of civilization had proceeded by the late twentieth century. Freud never reckoned with a world in which the loosening of constraint would lead to new and generally unperceived forms of manipulation. But there are other explanations of the distance which separates us from Freud. Whatever the solace provided by his reformulation of the idea of civilization, its multiple interpretations would continue to be buffeted by the horrors of the twentieth century: the rise of fascism, the stupidities and cruelties intrinsic to bureaucratic collectivism, another World War, Judeocide and other genocides, and the possibility of the extermination of the human race. So lauded as to become an item of cant by the end of the nineteenth century, the idea of civilization, despite the titles of our textbooks and courses, stands in much greater disrepute at the end of the twentieth century.[3] Given the ideological uses to which it was put in the past, perhaps that is as it should be.

Certainly some of the groups once excluded from civilization or relegated to its lower ranks, notably women and aborigines, have become more politically active. Reversing the process of equation from above, they have begun to forge at least tactical alliances among themselves. But they face the challenge of either emphasizing exclusiveness or demanding admission into the hallowed circle of what used to be known as civilization and what now might be described more mundanely as the power structure, a distinction which underscores how far we have travelled from civilization in a world where, on the whole, the ruling class no longer needs to buttress its position with claims to a superior culture. Both courses involve dangers. It is remarkable, for instance, the extent to which "essentialist" feminism involves simply a reversal of the male descriptions and prescriptions of the nineteenth century. On the other hand, entry into the power structure, on the basis of gender equality, will probably reinforce rather than transform that structure.[4]

The only group possibly capable of transforming that structure, the industrial working class, is today very much at risk. Not only have structural changes within capitalism weakened it in this period of post-Fordism, but it has been the victim of a savage class warfare waged from above during the past two decades. Reeling under these blows, it is indifferent to, if not actively opposed to, much of the more vocal agitations of today. But it will only be through the mobilization of the class directly tied to production and, hence, capable of stopping production, that the changes sought by the champions of surrogate proletariats will be effectuated in a meaningful manner. Short of such mobilization, the changes sought are likely to eventuate in a situation where neo-corporatist groups, often themselves ferociously divided internally, achieve rights at the expense of both the hard-pressed individual and a humanity more often invoked than, in several senses, realized.

If I yield to no one in my appreciation of Gothic cathedrals and respect for Thomas Aquinas, I am not enchanted with the prospect of a neo-medievalism, least of all an electronic medievalism.[5] Although there are signs that neo-corporatism is already becoming institutionalized, at least within the universities, the contemporary situation, sometimes described as postmodern, remains remarkably fluid. Novelties proliferate, but the genuinely new is nowhere to be found outside of Eastern Europe where, in yet another blow to the idea of progress, it bears an all too alarming resemblance to the old. It may well be that we have "gone primitive," that is, that we exist as "savage intellects leading modern lives."[6] Some glory in this situation. I am appalled by it.

All those named in the preface are eminently civilized in that eighteenth century sense of a refinement of manners. The charge brought against that definition, of course, was that it involved a high degree of artificiality. When contrasted with the authentic or the sincere, the charge is supposed to be damning. But there were any number of authentic or sincere Nazis. Hence, it would be better to recognize that all humans, shortly after birth, begin to acquire a second nature. If the biological constants shared with other animals remain, those constants become interpreted in cultural terms. This second nature, as displayed by individuals and societies, can be remarkably vicious: both Hobbes and Freud did a disservice to the wolf. More generally, whether lupine or bovine or whatever, animals are unencumbered by moral principles, the absence and presence of which in humans can lead to merciless cruelty. The basic point here, however, is that biological phenomena like birth, survival, sex and death are experienced by humans only through social institutions and value structures, some of which, though we are taught not to discriminate today, I find preferable to others. For instance, I find no reason to be especially patient with religious fundamentalists of any sort, in part because I know they have no intention of extending toleration to me, in part because their beliefs violate, to use Jürgen Habermas' terms, any notion of communicative rationality.

I am prepared to make such judgements in light of the values of the period in which the term "civilization" first appeared, the much-maligned Enlightenment. We now recognize, of course, its darker side. Understandable in terms of the time, its veneration of the instrumental reason of science led into the pseudo-science of biological racism, the rape of the environment, and the bomb, not to mention the mindless positivism of the Second and Third Internationals. Moreover, although the refinement of manners initially radiated from the courts and aristocracies, the development of civilization rested on an opulence and luxury which as its early theorists recognized and lauded, much to the disgust of sterner classical republicans, was tied to the growth of commerce. In brief, though perhaps inclined to pay more attention to exchange rather than production, these theorists found a link between civilization and capitalism. Genuine enough, that link rendered the notion of civilization open to crass appropriation by the philistine bourgeoisie of the following century.

These people were wedded to the preeminent value of control, especially the control of Nature, which in turn, entailed the control of human nature. That meant, first of all, the self-control which distinguished the civilized from the uncivilized or quasi-civilized. Perceived as closer to Nature, these latter groups, if only for their own good, had to be controlled. Such control, in the case of certain aboriginal groups, bordered on the possibility of extermination. With few exceptions, civilized men, precisely because they were civilized, seldom called for a policy of extermination. But a significant number of them were quite prepared to let Nature take what they accepted as its course in the contact between the materially and culturally superior and the primitives. But even here lines were drawn. If it was allowed that the Australian aborigines and the Amerindians might follow the Tasmanians into extinction, such groups were not deemed necessary to the physical labour upon which civilization rested. That was not the case with black Africans. Nor was it the case with the agricultural and industrial labourers of the countries perceived as civilized. Women, of course, were necessary to the reproduction of the species. With the number of mad multiplying and the sophistication of crime increasing, lunatics and criminals came to be accepted as inevitable accompaniments to civilization, with both to be treated by methods based directly or indirectly upon medical models.

The Enlightenment, in brief, has a lot to answer for, both in itself and in its consequences. Given the weight of the indictment against it, it is just as well that there can never be complete restorations in history, just as well that the past cannot wholly be recaptured or reconstructed. But that should not imply the abandonment of what Habermas has called "the project of modernity," the project of Enlightenment.[7] With reason central to that project, it is open to everybody (except for the severely mentally disabled) to participate in. That project now entails the immensely difficult task of forging for the first time a global civilization on grounds which have little to do with international rock festivals, let alone an international capitalist market.

At the risk of offending neo-romantic primitivists and other postmodernists, and fully aware of the dangers involved, I would insist that, if it is to be realized, Western rationality, in its variety of forms, will have to be central to this project. With the distinction between "pure" and "applied" science now almost wholly eclipsed, instrumental rationality has taken on a life of its own. If that life involves not only the manipulation of things but also the manipulation of humans as things, there is still a need for it. Given the size of the global population, it will be all the more necessary for preserving the natural environment and creating a social environment which provides simultaneously for basic security and maximum independence for all. But the dangers constituted by instrumental reason make all the more important the need for communicative or dialogic reason, that is, the ability of people to arrive at rational decisions through rational discussion, in order to prevent decisions being imposed upon them by "experts." But that, in turn, calls for the rehabilitation of dialectical reason which alone possesses the ability to reconcile the interests of specific cultural groups with a universal standard of human behaviour within the context of global civilization.

This argument will undoubtedly be qualified as ethnocentric by some and perhaps it is. I would insist, however, that the invitation to participation in these forms of reason remains open-ended and without coercion. All too often hitherto the assimilationist position represented a secularization of Augustine's "Compel them to come in." With its dangers fully exposed, there is now no reason for a patronizing tone of necessary superiority. If Westerners have much to teach, they also have much to learn. To see other people as subjects capable of forming their own destinies, and not as objects of scientistic investigation, is to begin to learn. It would be easier, of course, to let the Western-dominated market carry all before it. While liable in this century to implosion, this has been the course of civilization up until now.

Given what this century has witnessed and is witnessing, I am not especially sanguine about the realization of the project of modernity or Enlightenment. If nothing else, the apparent strength of capitalism and immense disparities in wealth it generates and sustains will continue to work against such a realization. We may be forced to settle for what we have or, indeed, for something worse. In any event, as Freud eventually came to realize sometime after Euclides de Cunha glimpsed it at the beginning of this century, "We are condemned to civilization."[8] The issue turns on what kind of a civilization we wish to inhabit and how much sacrifice and hard work it will require.

One does not have to discount the degree of exploitation entailed by scarcity to recognize that humans have been capable of marvellous creations. If some can still find consolation for the discontents engendered by civilization in Freud's powerful system of psychic metaphors, I prefer to find solace in a somewhat unlikely source. Although he lacked the term "civilization" and subordinated the coercive City of Man to the City of God, Augustine still declared: "Nevertheless, it is wrong to deny that the aims of human civilization [*civitas*] are good, for this is the highest end that mankind of itself can achieve."[9] He wrote at a time when the barbarians were at the gates and the Roman gods in flight. His City of God is now but a ruin, his deity but a spectre. We are left, consequently, with "the highest end" that humankind can achieve. To be fully civilized is to be fully human. The obstacles to the achievement of that goal, including a postmodern primitivism fostered by market and media, are truly formidable. But the effort must be made. Given what confronts us, the choice, in a manner totally unsuspected by the nineteenth century, may well be between civilization and extermination.

NOTES

1. Sigmund Freud, *The Question of Lay Analysis* (New York: W.W. Norton & Co., 1978), p. 44.
2. *Ibid.*, p. 38.
3. Any attempt to trace the history of the concept from Freud's essay of 1930 to the present would have to take into account such influential works as Arnold Toynbee's *A Study of History* and Herbert Marcuse's *Eros and Civilization.* Toynbee, incidently, found the beginnings of the postmodern in 1875.
4. While aimed at securing greater clarity with regard to a host of issues, current feminist theory runs the danger of becoming bogged down in dogmatism and acrimonious exchange. Two vital issues continue to demand concentrated attention. First, any interpretation of gender equality which departs from the goal of equal pay for equal work is likely to be a snare. Second, more must be done for single mothers.
5. Another sign of neo-medievalism resides in the importance of the corporate logo today. Under the bombardment of the electronic media, we are becoming more visually oriented and more illiterate. Signs and symbols, like language itself, can express and disguise power.
6. Marianna Torgovnick, *Gone Primitive: Savage Intellects, Modern Lives* (Chicago: University of Chicago Press, 1990), p. 246. Focused on the convoluted appeal of the primitive to highly sophisticated Westerners, this book in many respects complements my studies in the ideological uses of the notion of civilization.
7. Jürgen Habermas, "Modernity—An Incomplete Project," Hal Foster (ed.), *The Anti-Aesthetic: Essays on Postmodern Culture* (Port Townsend: Bay Press, 1983), pp. 3-15.
8. Euclides de Cunha, *Rebellion in the Backlands* (Chicago: University of Chicago Press, 1944), p. 54. While fascinating as a compendium of the misplaced lore of social science at the beginning of the century, this great book describes, in the Brazilian context, problems now being confronted globally.
9. Augustine of Hippo, *The City of God* (Garden City: Image Books, 1958), p. 327.

BIBLIOGRAPHY

PRIMARY SOURCES

Acton, William. *Prostitution*. New York: Frederick A. Praeger, 1968.

Adams, Henry. *The Education of Henry Adams*. New York: Modern Library, 1931.

Arnold, Matthew. *Culture & Anarchy*. Cambridge: Cambridge University Press, 1960.

___. "Civilization in the United States," *The Complete Works of Matthew Arnold*, IX. Ann Arbor: University of Michigan Press, 1977. pp. 350-69.

___. "Equality," Lionel Trilling, ed. *The Portable Matthew Arnold*. New York: The Viking Press, 1949.

___. "Friendship's Garland (Part I)," *The Complete Works of Matthew Arnold*, V. Ann Arbor: University of Michigan Press, 1965. pp. 1-77

Augustine of Hippo. *The City of God*. Garden City: Image Books, 1958.

Bagehot, Walter. "Physics and Politics." *The Collected Works of Walter Bagehot*. VII. London: The Economist, 1974. pp. 17-144.

Bell, Clive. "Civilization," *Civilization and Old Friends*. Chicago: University of Chicago Press, 1973. pp. 5-189.

Bloch, Iwan. *The Sexual Life of Our Time in Its Relations to Modern Civilization*. New York: Allied Book Co., 1926.

Booth, General (William). *In Darkest England and the Way Out*. London: International Headquarters of the Salvation Army, 1980.

Boswell, James. *Life of Johnson*. London: Oxford University Press, 1969.

Breecher, Jonathan and Richard Bienvenu, (eds.), *The Utopian Vision of Charles Fourier: Selected Texts on Work, Love, and Passionate Attraction*. Boston: Beacon Press, 1971.

Buckle, Henry Thomas. *History of Civilization in England*, I-III. London: Longmans, Green & Co., 1908.

___. "The Influence of Women and the Progress of Knowledge," *Essays*. New York: D. Appleton and Co., 1863.

Catlin, George. *North American Indians*. London: Penguin Books, 1989.

Coleridge, Samuel Taylor. *On the Constitution of the Church and State, Collected Works*, X. Princeton: Princeton University Press, 1976.

Cochran, Thomas C., (ed.), *The New American State Papers: Indian Affairs: General*, II. Washington: Scholarly Resources, 1972.

Comte, Auguste. "Plan of the Scientific Operations Necessary for Reorganizing Society," Gertrud Lenzer, (ed.), *Auguste Comte and Positivism: The Essential Writings.* New York: Harper & Row, 1975. pp. 9-67.

___. "Cours de Philosophie Positive," Gertrud Lenzer, (ed.), *Auguste Comte and Positivism: The Essential Writings.* New York: Harper & Row, 1975. pp. 71-306.

Cromer, The Earl of. *Modern Egypt*, I-II. New York: Macmillan, 1901.

Cunha, Euclides de. *Rebellion in the Backlands.* Chicago: University of Chicago Press, 1944.

Darwin, Charles. *The Voyage of the Beagle.* New York: Bantam Books, 1958.

___. "The Descent of Man," *The Origin of Species by Means of Natural Selection or the Preservation of Favoured Races in the Struggle for Life and The Descent of Man and Selection in Relation to Sex.* New York: The Modern Library, n.d. pp. 389-924.

de Condorcet, Marie J.A.M. *Sketch for a Historical Picture of the Progress of the Human Mind.* London: Wiedenfeld and Nicolson, 1955.

de Custine, Marquis. *Empire of the Czar: A Journey Through Eternal Russia.* New York: Anchor Books, 1989.

de Gobineau, Arthur. *Essai sur l'inégalité des races humaines.* Paris: Editions Pierre Belfond, 1967.

de Goncourt, Edmund, "Journal," Roland N. Stomberg (ed.), *Realism, Naturalism and Symbolism: Modes of Thought and Expression in Europe, 1848-1914,* New York: Harper Torchbooks, 1968. pp. 71-91.

de Saussure, Leopold. "Psychologie de colonisation française dans ses rapports avec les sociétés indigènes," Philip D. Curtin, (ed.) *Imperialism.* New York: Harper & Row, 1971. pp. 85-92.

de Tocqueville, Alexis. *Democracy in America*, I-II. New York: Vintage Books, 1959.

___. *"The European Revolution" & Correspondence with Gobineau.* Garden City: Anchor Books, 1959.

___. "Journeys to England and Ireland," Christopher Hervie, Graham Martin and Aaron Scharf, (eds.) *Industrialization & Culture, 1830-1914.* Glasgow: Macmillan and Co., 1970.

du Camp, Maxime. *Les convulsions de Paris*, IV, *La Commune à l'Hotel de Ville.* Paris: Hachette, 1881.

Durkheim, Emile. *Suicide: A Study in Sociology.* New York: Free Press, 1951.

Ellis, Havelock. *Studies in the Psychology of Sex*, I. New York: Random House, 1942.

___. *Studies in the Psychology of Sex*, II. New York: Random House, 1936.

Emerson, Ralph Waldo. "Civilization," *Society and Solitude.* Boston: Houghton Mifflin and Co., 1904. pp. 17-34.

Engels, Frederick. *The Origin of the Family, Private Property, and the State.* New York: Pathfinder Press, 1972.

___ . "French Rule in Algeria," Schlomo Avineri, (ed.) *Karl Marx on Colonialism and Modernization.* Garden City: Anchor Books, 1969. pp. 47-48.

Esquerol, Jean Etienne. "Mental Maladies. A Treatise on Insanity," Charles Goshen, (ed.) *A Documentary History of Psychiatry: A Source Book on Historical Principles.* London: Vision Press, 1967. pp. 315-69.

Freud, Sigmund and Joseph Breuer. *Studies in Hysteria.* Harmondsworth: Penguin Books, 1974.

Freud, Sigmund. *Beyond the Pleasure Principle.* New York: W.W. Norton & Co., 1961.

___ . *Civilization and Its Discontents.* New York: W.W. Norton & Co., 1961.

___ . *Five Lectures on Psycho-Analysis.* New York: W.W. Norton & Co., 1989.

___ . *Group Psychology and the Analysis of the Ego.* New York: W.W. Norton & Co., 1959.

___ . *Introductory Lectures on Psychoanalysis.* Harmondsworth: Penguin Books, 1973.

___ . *Jokes and Their Relation to the Unconscious.* Harmondsworth: Penguin Books, 1976.

___ . *New Introductory Lectures.* New York: W.W. Norton & Co., 1965.

___ . *The Future of an Illusion.* Garden City: Doubleday and Co., 1964.

___ . *The Interpretation of Dreams.* Harmondsworth: Penguin Books, 1976.

___ . *The Psychopathology of Everyday Life.* Harmondsworth: Penguin Books, 1976.

___ . *The Question of Lay Analysis.* New York: W.W. Norton & Co., 1978.

___ . "'Civilized' Sexual Morality and Modern Nervous Illness," *Civilization, Society and Religion.* Harmondsworth: Penguin Books, 1985. pp. 33-55.

___ . "Dora," *Case Histories, I, Dora and Little Hans.* Harmondsworth: Penguin Books, 1977. pp. 31-164.

___ . "Some Psychical Consequences of the Anatomical Distinction Between the Sexes," *On Sexuality.* Harmondsworth: Penguin Books, 1977. pp. 323-43.

___ . "Thoughts for the Times on War and Death," *Civilization, Society and Religion.* Harmondsworth: Penguin Books, 1985. pp. 57-89.

___ . "Three Essays on Sexuality," *On Sexuality.* Harmondsworth: Penguin Books, 1977. pp. 33-169.

___ . "Totem and Taboo," *The Origin of Religion.* Harmondsworth: Penguin Books, 1985. pp. 43-224.

Freud, Ernst, (ed.) *The Letters of Sigmund Freud.* New York: Basic Books, 1975.

Fried, Albert and Richard M. Elman, (eds.) *Charles Booth's London. A Portrait of the Poor at the Turn of the Century, Drawn from His "Life and Labour of the People in London."* London: Hutchison, 1969.

Funck-Brentano, Th. *La Civilization et ses lois morales sociales.* Paris, E. Plon et Cie., 1876.

Galantière, Lewis, (ed.) *The Goncourt Journals.* Garden City: Doubleday Anchor Books, 1958.

Gibbon, Edward. *The History of the Decline and Fall of the Roman Empire*, I-III. New York: Heritage Press, 1946.

Greeley, Horace. "An Overland Journey from New York to San Francisco," Black, Nancy B. and Bette S. Wiedman (eds.), *White on Red: Images of the American Indian.* Port Washington: Kennikat Press, 1976. pp. 257-60.

Gross, Hans. *Criminal Psychology. A Manual for Judges, Practitioners, and Students.* Boston: Little, Brown and Co., 1911.

Guizot, François. "The History of Civilization in Europe," Mellon, Stanley (ed.), *Guizot: Historical Essays and Lectures.* Chicago: University of Chicago Press, 1977. pp. 140- 265.

___. "The History of Civilization in France," Mellon, Stanley, (ed.), *Guizot: Historical Essays and Lectures.* Chicago: University of Chicago Press, 1977. pp. 266-394.

Habermas, Jürgen. "Modernity—An Incomplete Project," Foster, Hal, (ed.), *The Anti-Aesthetic: Essays on Postmodern Culture.* Port Townsend: Bay Press, 1983. pp. 3-15.

Hall, Charles. *The Effects of Civilization on the People in European States.* London: T. Ostell and C. Chappel, 1805.

Hall, G. Stanley. *Adolescence: Its Psychology and Its Relations to Physiology, Anthropology, Sociology, Sex, Crime, Religion and Education*, I-II. New York: New York Times, 1969.

Hartmann, Eduard von. *Philosophy of the Unconscious. Speculative Results According to the Inductive Method of Psychical Science,* II. London: Kegan Paul, Trench, Trüber & Co., 1831.

Huxley, Thomas Henry. "Emancipation—Black and White," *Lay Sermons, Addresses and Reviews*, New York: D. Appleton & Co., 1871. pp. 20-26.

Itard, Jean-Marc-Gaspard. *The Wild Boy of Aveyron (Rapports et mémoires sur le sauvage de l'Aveyron).* New York: The Century Co., 1932.

James, Sr., Henry. "Socialism and Civilization," Matthiessen, F. O., *The James Family.* New York: Vintage Books, 1980. pp. 40-58.

Kidd, Benjamin. *The Control of the Tropics.* New York: Macmillan Co., 1898.

Kingsley, Mary H. *Travels in West Africa.* London: Frank Cass & Co., Ltd., 1965.

Le Bon, Gustave. *La Psychologie politique et la Défense sociale.* Paris: Flammarion, n.d.

___. *Les Civilisations de l'Inde.* Paris: Librairie de Firmin-Didot et Cie., 1887.

___. *Psychologie des foules.* Paris: Presses universitaires de France, 1963.

___. *The French Revolution and the Psychology of Revolution.* New Brunswick: Transaction Books, 1980.

___. "Aphorisms of the Present Time," Widener, Alice, (ed.), *Gustave Le Bon: The Man and His Works.* Indianapolis: Liberty Press, 1979. pp. 267-306.

Lecky, William E. H. *History of European Morals from Augustus to Charlemagne.* New York: George Braziller, 1955.

Le Play, F. *La Méthode sociale.* Tours: Alfred Mame et fils, 1879.

Lombroso, Cesare. *Crime. Its Causes and Remedies.* Boston: Little, Brown and Co., 1911.

Lombroso, Cesare and William Ferro, *The Female Offender.* NewYork: D. Appleton and Co., 1897.

Malthus, Thomas R. *An Essay on the Principle of Population.* New York: W.W. Norton & Co., 1976.

Mann, Thomas. *Reflections of an Unpolitical Man.* New York: Frederick Unger, 1983.

Marx, Karl. "The British Rule in India," Scholmo Avineri, (ed.), *Karl Marx on Colonialism and Modernization.* Garden City: Anchor Books, 1969.

Masaryk, Thomas G. *Suicide and the Meaning of Civilization.* Chicago: University of Chicago Press, 1970.

Masson, Jeffrey M., (ed.) *The Complete Letters of Sigmund Freud to Wilhelm Fliess.* Cambridge: Harvard University Press, 1985.

Masterman, C.F.G. *The Condition of England.* London: Methuen & Co., 1960.

Maudsley, Henry. *The Pathology of Mind.* London: Macmillam and Co., 1879.

___ . *Responsibility in Mental Disease.* London: Kegan Paul, Trench, Trübner and Co., 1892.

Mayhew, Henry. *London Labour and the London Poor,* I-IV. New York: Dover Publications, 1968.

McGuire, William, (ed.) *The Freud / Jung Letters: The Correspondence between Sigmund Freud and C.G. Jung.* Princeton: Princeton University Press, 1974.

Michelet, Jules. *The People.* Urbana: University of Illinois Press, 1973.

Mill, James. *The History of British India.* Chicago: University of Chicago Press, 1975.

Mill, John Stuart. *Principles of Political Economy with Some of Their Applications to Social Philosophy.* Books III-IV, *Collected Works,* III. Toronto: University of Toronto Press, 1965.

___ . *A System of Logic, Ratiocinative and Inductive; Being a Connected View of the Principles of Evidence and the Methods of Scientific Method,* Books IV-VI, *Collected Works* VIII. Toronto: University of Toronto Press, 1974.

___ . "Civilization," *Essays on Politics and Culture.* Garden City: Doubleday and Co.,1962. pp. 51-84.

___ . "Modern French Historical Works," *Essays on French History and Historians, Collected Works,* XX. Toronto: University of Toronto Press, 1985. pp. 15-52.

___ . "Representative Government," *Utilitarianism, Liberty, Representative Government.* New York: E. P. Dutton, 1951.

Morgan, Lewis Henry. *Ancient Society, or Researches in the Lines of Human Progress From Savagery Through Barbarism to Civilization.* Cleveland: Meridian Books, 1963.

Newman, John Henry. *The Idea of a University*. Garden City: Image Books, 1959.

Park, Mungo. *Travels in the Interior Districts of Africa*. London: M. Dent & Sons, 1907.

Pfeiffer, Ernst, (ed.) *Sigmund Freud and Lou Andreas Salomé*. New York: W.W. Norton & Co., 1985.

Prichard, James Cowles. *Researches into the Physical History of Man*. Chicago: University of Chicago Press, 1973.

Rawlinson, Sir Henry. *England and Russia in the East: A Series of Papers on the Political and Geographical Condition of Central Asia* New York: Praeger, 1970.

Renan, Ernst. "L'Avenir de la Science," *Oeuvres completes*, III. Paris: Calmann-Levy, n.d. pp. 715-1121.

Schapera, I., (ed.), *Livingstone's Missionary Correspondence, 1841-1856*. Berkeley: University of California Press, 1961.

Seeley, J. R. *The Expansion of England*. Chicago: University of Chicago Press, 1971.

Simmel, Georg. *On Women, Sexuality, and Love*. New Haven: Yale University Press, 1984.

Smith, Adam. *An Inquiry into the Nature and Causes of the Wealth of Nations*, I-II. Indianapolis: Liberty Classics, 1961.

Spencer, Herbert. *The Principles of Psychology*, I. Boston: Longwood Press, 1977.

Spengler, Oswald. *The Decline of the West*. New York: The Modern Library, 1962.

Stanley, Henry M. *In Darkest Africa or the Quest, Rescue and Retreat of Emin, Governor of Equatoria*. London: Sampson, Low, Marston, Seark and Remington, 1890.

Strong, Josiah. *Our Country; Its Possible Future and the Present Crisis*. Cambridge: Belnap Press, 1963.

Tarde, Gabriel. *Penal Philosophy*. Boston: Little, Brown and Co., 1912.

Taylor, W. Cooke. *Notes of a Tour of the Manufacturing Districts of Lancashire*. London: Frank Cass and Co., 1968.

Twain, Mark. "To the Person Sitting in Darkness," Bernard de Voto, (ed.), *The Portable Mark Twain*. New York: Penguin Books, 1977.

Tylor, Edward B. *The Origins of Culture*, I-II. New York: Harper & Row, 1958.

Valéry, Paul. *History and Politics, Collected Works*, X. New York: Bollingen Foundation, 1962. pp. 23-36.

Wallace, Alfred R. *A Narrative of Travels on the Amazon and Rio Negro, with an Account of the Native Tribes, and Observations on the Climate, Geology and Natural History of the Amazon Valley*. London: Ward, Lock & Bowden, Ltd., 1895.

___ . *The Malay Archipelago: The Land of the Orang-utan and the Bird of Paradise, A Narrative of Travel, with Studies of Man and Nature*. London: Macmillan and Co., 1922.

Bibliography

SECONDARY SOURCES

Annan, Noel. *Leslie Stephen: The Godless Victorian*. New York: Random House, 1984.

Becker, Howard and Harry Elmer Barnes. *Social Thought from Lore to Science: A History and Interpretation of Man's Ideas about Life with His Fellows*. I-II. Washington: Harren Press, 1952.

Bénéton, Philippe. *Histoire de mots: culture et civilisation*. Paris: Presses de la Fondation nationale des Sciences politiques, 1975.

Benveniste, Emile. *Problems in General Linguistics*. Coral Gables: University of Miami Press, 1971.

Bernheimer, Charles. *Figures of Ill Repute: Representing Prostitution in Nineteenth Century France*. Cambridge: Harvard University Press, 1989.

Berlin, Isaiah. *Russian Thinkers*. Harmondsworth: Penguin Books, 1979.

Bolt, Christine. *Victorian Attitudes to Race*. London: Routledge & Kegan Paul, 1971.

Briggs, Asa. *Victorian Cities*. Harmondsworth: Pelican Books, 1968.

Brodie, Fawn M. *The Devil Drives: A Life of Sir Richard Burton*. New York: Ballentyne Books, 1969.

Brunschwig, Henri. *French Colonialism, 1871-1914: Myths and Realities*. New York: Frederick A. Praeger, 1964.

Burns, Edward McNall. *The American Idea Of Mission: Concepts of National Purpose and Destiny*. New Brunswick: Rutgers University Press, 1957.

Bury, J. B. *The Idea of Progress: An Inquiry into Its Origin and Growth*. New York: Dover Publications, 1955.

Cairns, H. Alan C. *Prelude to Imperialism: British Reactions to Central African Society, 1840-1890*. London: Routledge & Kegan Paul, 1965.

Chevalier, Louis. *Laboring Classes and Dangerous Classes in Paris During the First Half of the Nineteenth Century*. Princeton: Princeton University Press, 1981.

Clark, Ronald W. *Freud: The Man and the Cause*. New York: Random House. 1980.

Cohen, William B. *The French Encounter with Africans; White Responses to Blacks, 1530-1880*. Bloomington: Indiana University Press, 1980.

Collie, Michael. *Henry Maudsley, Victorian Psychiatrist: A Bibliographical Study*. Winchester: St. Paul's Bibliographies, 1988.

Dawson, Raymond. *The Chinese Chameleon: an analysis of European conceptions of Chinese civilization*. London: Oxford University Press, 1967.

Dinnerstein, Leonard; Roger Nicols and David M. Reimers. *Natives and Strangers: Ethnic Groups and the Building of America*. New York: Oxford University Press, 1979.

Dippie, Brian W. *The Vanishing American. White Attitudes and U.S. Indian Policy*. Middletown: Wesleyan University Press, 1982.

Drinnon, Richard. *Facing West: The Metaphysics of Indian-Hating and Empire Building*. Minneapolis: University of Minnesota Press, 1980.

Duchet, Michèle. *Anthropologie et Histoire du siècle des lumières*. Paris: François Maspero, 1971.

Ekstein, Modris. *The Rites of Spring: The Great War and the Birth of the Modern Age*. Toronto: Lester and Ospen Dennys, 1989.

Elias, Norbert. *The Civilizing Process*, I-II, Oxford: Basil Blackwell, 1978.

Febvre, Lucien. "'Civilisation':" Evolution of a Word and a Group of Ideas," Peter Burke, (ed.), *A New King of History, From the Writings of Lucien Febvre*. London: Routledge & Kegan Paul, 1973. pp. 219-57.

Field, H. John. *Toward a Programme of Imperial Life: The British Empire at the Turn of the Century*. Westport: Greenwood Press, 1982.

Foucault, Michel. *Discipline and Punish: The Birth of the Prison*. New York: Vintage Books, 1977.

Gallagher, Catherine and Laqueur, Thomas. *The Making of the Modern Body: Sexuality and Society in the Nineteenth Century*. Berkeley: University of California Press, 1986.

Gasman, David. *The Scientific Origin of National Socialism: Social Darwinism in Ernst Haekel and the German Monist League*. London: Macdonald, 1971.

Gerbi, Antonelle. *The Dispute of the New World: The History of a Polemic, 1750-1900*. Pittsburgh: University of Pittsburgh Press, 1973.

Girardet, Raoul. *L'idée coloniale en France de 1871 à 1962*. Paris: La Table Ronde, 1972.

Goldstein, Jan. *Console and Classify: The French Psychiatric Profession in the Nineteenth Century*. Cambridge: Cambridge University Press, 1987.

Harris, Marvin. *The Rise of Anthropological Theory: A History of Theories of Culture*. New York: Thomas Y. Cromwell Co., 1968.

Herbert, Christopher. *Culture and Anomie: Ethnographic Imagination in the Nineteenth Century*. Chicago: University of Chicago Press, 1991.

Himmelfarb, Gertrude. *The Idea of Poverty: England in the Early Industrial Age*. New York: Alfred Knopf, 1989.

Horseman, Reginald. *Race and Manifest Destiny: The Origins of American Racial Anglo-Saxonism*. Cambridge: Harvard University Press, 1981.

Hynes, Samuel. *The Edwardian Turn of Mind*. Princeton: Princeton University Press, 1968.

Ignatieff, Michael. *A Just Measure of Pain: The Penitentiary in the Industrial Revolution. 1750-1850*. London: Penguin Books, 1989.

Jones, Garth Stedman. *Outcast London: A Study in the Relationship between Classes in Victorian Society*. Oxford: Clarendon Press, 1971.

Kiernan, V. G. *The Lords of Human Kind: European Attitudes to the Outside World in the Imperial Age*. Harmondsworth: Penguin Books, 1972.

Bibliography

Kohn, Hans. *Pan-Slavism: Its History and Ideology*. New York: Vintage Books, 1960.

Kroeber, A. L. and Clyde Kluckhohn. *Culture: A Critical Review of Concepts and Definitions*. New York: Vintage Books, n.d.

Laffey, John F. "Cacophonic Rites: Modernism and Postmodernism," *Historical Reflections / Réflexions historiques*, 14, 1. Spring, 1987. pp. 1-32.

Lears, T. J. Jackson. *No Place of Grace: Antimodernism and the Transformation of American Culture, 1880-1920*. New York: Pantheon Books, 1981.

Lees, Andrew. *Cities Perceived: Urban Society in European and American Thought, 1820-1940*. New York: Columbia University Press, 1985.

Lorimer, Douglas A. *Colour, Class and the Victorians: English Attitudes to the Negro in the Mid-Nineteenth Century*. Leicester: Leicester University Press, 1978.

Marcus, Steven. *Engels, Manchester, and the Working Class*. New York: Random House, 1974.

Masson, Jeffrey. *The Assault on Truth: Freud's Suppression of the Seduction Theory*. New York: Farrar, Straus and Giroux, 1984.

McClelland, Robert. *The Heathen Chinese: A Study of American Attitudes toward China, 1890-1905*. Columbus: Ohio State University Press, 1971.

Merk, Frederick. *Manifest Destiny and Mission in American History*. New York: Alfred A Knopf, 1963.

Michel, Pierre. *Les Barbares, 1789-1848: Un Mythe romantique*. Lyon: Presses universitaires de Lyon, 1981.

Murphey, Rhoads. *The Outsiders: The Western Experience in India and China*. Ann Arbor: University of Michigan Press, 1977.

Normandeau, André. "Charles Lucas (1803-1850)," Hermann Mannheim, (ed.), *Pioneers in Criminology*. Montclair: Patterson Smith, 1972. pp. 138-57.

Panichas, George A., (ed.), *Promise of Greatness: The War of 1914-1918*. New York: The John Day Co., 1968.

Pearce, Roy Henry. *The Savages of America: A Study of the Indian and the Idea of Civilization*. Baltimore: The Johns Hopkins Press, 1968.

Richardson, Ruth. *Death, Dissection and the Destitute*. Harmondsworth: Penguin Books, 1988.

Romein, Jan. *The Watershed of Two Worlds: Europe in 1900*. Middletown: Wesleyan University Press, 1978.

Rosen, George. *Madness in Society. Chapters in the Historical Sociology of Mental Illness*. New York: Harper Torchbooks, 1969.

Rudorff, Raymond. *The Belle Epoque: Paris in the Nineties*. New York: Saturday Review Press, 1973.

Showalter, Elaine. "Victorian Women and Insanity," Andrew Scull, (ed.), *Madhouses, Mad-Doctors, and Madmen. The Social History of Psychiatry in the Victorian Era*. Philadelphia: University of Pennsylvania Press, 1981. pp. 313-38.

Soltau, Roger Henry. *French Political Thought in the Nineteenth Century.* New York: Russell & Russell, 1959.

Stocking, Jr., George W. *Race, Culture, and Evolution: Essays in the History of Anthropology.* New York: Free Press, 1968.

___. *Victorian Anthropology.* New York: Free Press, 1987.

Strachey, Lytton. *Queen Victoria.* New York: Harcourt, Brace & World, 1921.

Thompson, E. P. *William Morris: From Romantic to Revolutionary.* London: Merlin Press, 1977.

Torgovnick, Marianna. *Gone Primitive: Savage Intellects, Modern Lives.* Chicago: University of Chicago Press, 1990.

Utley, Robert M. *The Indian Frontier of the American West, 1846-1890.* Albuquerque: University of New Mexico Press, 1984.

Veith, Ilza. *Hysteria: The History of a Disease.* Chicago: University of Chicago Press, 1965.

Weber, Eugen. *Peasants into Frenchmen. The Modernization of Rural France.* Stanford: Stanford University Press, 1976.

Williams, Raymond. *Culture and Society, 1780-1950.* Harmondsworth: Penguin Books, 1961.

___. *Keywords. A Vocabulary of Culture and Society.* New York: Oxford University Press, 1983.

___. "Culture and Civilization," Paul Edwards, (ed.), *The Encyclopedia of Philosophy,* II. New York: Macmillan Publishing Co., 1967. pp. 273-76.

Young, G. M. *Victorian England: Portrait of an Age.* New York: Oxford University Press, 1964.

Zeldin, Theodore. *France, 1848-1945, II, Intellect, Taste and Anxiety.* Oxford: Clarendon Press, 1977.

INDEX

Also published by

BLACK ROSE BOOKS

RETHINKING CAMELOT
JFK, the Vietnam War, and US Political Culture
Noam Chomsky

A thorough analysis of JFK's role in the US invasion of Vietnam and a probing reflection of the elite political culture that allowed and encouraged the Cold War. Chomsky dismisses the American myth portraying JFK as a shining knight promising peace, foiled only by assassins bent on stopping this lone hero who would have unilaterally withdrawn from Vietnam had he lived. Instead, the thesis offered is that US institutions and American political culture, not individual presidents, are the key to understanding the US and its behaviour.

200 pages
Paperback ISBN: 1-895431-72-7 $19.95
Hardcover ISBN: 1-895431-73-5 $38.95
International Politics/History

IMAGINING THE MIDDLE EAST
Thierry Hentsch
Translated by Fred A. Reed

Winner of the 1992 English-language Governor General's Literary Award for Translation

Thierry Hentsch examines how the Western perception of the Middle East was formed and how we have used these perceptions as a rationalization for setting policies and determining actions. He sees our ideas of the other and our ethnocentrism not simply as innocent myopia but as our whole way of viewing the world. He believes that the Middle East serves as a mirror to the Western consciousness, as a point of reference – changing form, contradictory, varying to the dictates of circumstance. The book concludes with the consequence of this imagination on the Gulf war and its aftermath.

218 pages, index
Paperback ISBN: 1-895431-12-3 $19.95
Hardcover ISBN: 1-895431-13-1 $38.95
L.C. No. 91-72982
International Politics/Cultural Studies

WHEN FREEDOM WAS LOST
The Unemployed, the Agitator, and the State
Lorne Brown

Backbreaking work for slave wages in labour camps — that was the government's response to thousands of young men looking for jobs in the Dirty Thirties.

Lorne Brown seeks to remedy the dearth of the 30s labour Canadiana with this study of little-known labour camps.

Books in Canada

208 pages, photographs
Paperback ISBN: 0-920057-77-2 $14.95
Hardcover ISBN: 0-920057-75-6 $36.95
History/Labour Studies

THE UNKNOWN REVOLUTION
Voline

A famous history of the Russian revolution and its aftermath. It reinstates material that has been omitted from recent editions of the English-language version and reproduces the complete text of the original French volumes.

The uniqueness of his work consists not only in the events that the author has selected for analysis, but also in the anarchist point of view...neither...would be found in the Soviet or Western academic literature of the Revolution.

Choice Magazine

717 pages, illustrated
Paperback ISBN: 0-919618-25-1 $19.95
Hardcover ISBN: 0-919618-26-6 $38.95
History

THE BITTER THIRTIES IN QUÉBEC
Evelyn Dumas

By examining, through the tradition of oral history, several strikes in the thirties and forties in transportation, textiles and other important industries, and by recording the impressions and feelings of some of the surviving strikers, Dumas has written a vivid, personalized history of the Québec labour situation during the Depression.

As enjoyable as a good adventure story... Thoroughly factual, yet written in lively journalistic style.

Globe and Mail

157 pages
Paperback ISBN: 0-919618-54-5 $7.95
Hardcover ISBN: 0-919618-53-7 $16.95
History/Labour Studies

EMMA GOLDMAN
Sexuality and the Impurity of the State
Bonnie Haaland

This book focuses on the *ideas* of Emma Goldman as they relate to the centrality of sexuality and reproduction. These ideas, on the liberatory potential of women's sexuality — birth control, voluntary motherhood, homosexual rights and the aggressive nature of marriage, religion and the State — are relevant to the current feminist debates on sexuality's pleasures, rather than its dangers, and as such, equates women's freedom with sexual freedom.

240 pages
Paperback ISBN: 1-895431-64-6 $19.95
Hardcover ISBN: 1-895431-65-4 $38.95
Women's Studies/Psychology/Sociology

WOMEN AND COUNTER-POWER
edited by Yolande Cohen

...these scholarly essays document women's political activity in anti-establishment movements, both historical and recent, in some of the nations peripheral to the powerful Western democracies and the USSR...The authors'...material provides information, as well as insights, not readily available elsewhere.

Small Press

244 pages
Paperback ISBN: 0-921689-10-1 $19.95
Hardcover ISBN: 0-921689-11-X $39.95
Women's Studies/International Politics

RACE ,GENDER AND WORK
A Multi-Cultural Economic History of Women in the United States
Teresa Amott and Julie Matthaei

...a detailed, richly textured history of American working women. And that's women plural — Indian, Chicana, European American, Asian American, African American, and Puerto Rican. Almost everyone will find a bit of her grandmother's own struggles and contributions in this impressively comprehensive book.

Barbara Ehrenreich author of *The Worst Years of Our Lives*

433 pages, index, appendices
Paperback ISBN: 0-921689-90-X $19.95
Hardcover ISBN: 0-921689-91-8 $38.95
Women's Studies\Labour Studies\Economics